D0929678

Additional praise for *Money Made Easy*

"If you've been feeling stuck in a rut with your money, then this book is your road map to financial security. *Money Made Easy* will both inspire and equip you to take your current financial situation to the next level, no matter where you are starting from."

—Talaat and Tai McNeely,
His and Her *Money* (www.hisandhermoney.com)

"*Money Made Easy* is an encouraging, deeply relatable detailed guide to financial success. It's a financial multivitamin."

—Julien and Kiersten Saunders,
authors of *Cashing Out: Win the Wealth Game by Walking Away*

MONEY MADE EASY

MONEY MADE EASY

How to Budget, Pay Off Debt, and Save Money

ALLISON BAGGERLY

WILEY

Copyright © 2023 by Allison Baggerly. All rights reserved.

Published by John Wiley & Sons, Inc., Hoboken, New Jersey.
Published simultaneously in Canada.

No part of this publication may be reproduced, stored in a retrieval system, or transmitted in any form or by any means, electronic, mechanical, photocopying, recording, scanning, or otherwise, except as permitted under Section 107 or 108 of the 1976 United States Copyright Act, without either the prior written permission of the Publisher, or authorization through payment of the appropriate per-copy fee to the Copyright Clearance Center, Inc., 222 Rosewood Drive, Danvers, MA 01923, (978) 750-8400, fax (978) 750-4470, or on the web at www.copyright.com. Requests to the Publisher for permission should be addressed to the Permissions Department, John Wiley & Sons, Inc., 111 River Street, Hoboken, NJ 07030, (201) 748-6011, fax (201) 748-6008, or online at http://www.wiley.com/go/permission.

Trademarks: Wiley and the Wiley logo are trademarks or registered trademarks of John Wiley & Sons, Inc. and/or its affiliates in the United States and other countries and may not be used without written permission. All other trademarks are the property of their respective owners. John Wiley & Sons, Inc. is not associated with any product or vendor mentioned in this book.

Limit of Liability/Disclaimer of Warranty: While the publisher and author have used their best efforts in preparing this book, they make no representations or warranties with respect to the accuracy or completeness of the contents of this book and specifically disclaim any implied warranties of merchantability or fitness for a particular purpose. No warranty may be created or extended by sales representatives or written sales materials. The advice and strategies contained herein may not be suitable for your situation. You should consult with a professional where appropriate. Further, readers should be aware that websites listed in this work may have changed or disappeared between when this work was written and when it is read. Neither the publisher nor authors shall be liable for any loss of profit or any other commercial damages, including but not limited to special, incidental, consequential, or other damages.

For general information on our other products and services or for technical support, please contact our Customer Care Department within the United States at (800) 762-2974, outside the United States at (317) 572-3993 or fax (317) 572-4002.

Wiley also publishes its books in a variety of electronic formats. Some content that appears in print may not be available in electronic formats. For more information about Wiley products, visit our web site at www.wiley.com.

Library of Congress Cataloging-in-Publication Data is Available:

ISBN 9781119894964 (Hardback)
ISBN 9781119894971 (ePDF)
ISBN 9781119894988 (ePub)

Cover Design: Wiley
Cover Images: © Nadiinko/Getty Images
Author photo: © Allison Baggerly

SKY10042654_021323

To my husband, Matt. Your encouragement and belief in what I can do never wavers. Thank you for that.

Table of Contents

Preface

I'm guessing you grabbed this book because you feel stuck with your money. Maybe your parents never taught you *how* to manage money properly because they were trying to figure it out along the way. Chances are you didn't learn about personal finances in school either.

Fast-forward to today, and here you are: holding this book, knowing deep down you want to be better with your money. You want to be able to pay off debt, take a family vacation, *and* save for retirement. You don't want your stomach to drop every time your beloved dog has an unexpected vet visit or your electricity bill is higher than you had anticipated.

Ultimately, you want peace of mind when it comes to your money. You want the freedom that managing your money well offers you.

I get it, and I've been there before. Years ago, I stood exactly where you are: holding a book, searching for answers. I wanted to know how I could change my money habits so I didn't feel *stuck* all the time.

To be honest, I didn't ever think I'd end up here—writing a book about how to make money easy. Mostly because money *wasn't* easy for me. I made a lot of mistakes with money, some of which you'll learn about in the pages of this book. But I also learned a *lot* of lessons. Lessons that taught me how I could have a positive relationship with my money and my budget and love my life in the process.

This book will offer you a step-by-step system to make money easy once and for all. You will be encouraged to look at your money through a completely different lens than before. You'll be challenged to question what society tells you is "right" about money and set goals that motivate you to make amazing financial progress.

No matter where you stand with money, this book is for you. The stories within these pages will inspire you, and the information will help you change your relationship with money for good. This is just the beginning!

Acknowledgments

This book wouldn't be a reality without the support of my husband, Matt. Thank you for believing in me, cheering me on, and supporting this big, crazy goal. Without you, our story would just be a daydream. I look around at the life we've built, and I can't help but remember what you said many years ago...*This will do.*

To my children, Evan and James. You are both the reason I wanted to change my life for the better. At the time, I did it for you. But you have both taught me that I alone am worthy of change. Evan, thank you for offering to write chapter 5 for me. James, thank you for the endless hugs when I was doubting myself. As I always say: you both make my heart happy.

To my parents, your endless support and help does not go unnoticed. Thank you for offering to step in when I need extra help. Mom, thank you for being my biggest cheerleader of all. You believe in me even when I don't believe in myself. My greatest goal is to be the type of mother for my children that you are to me.

To Amanda, you have been there to listen and encourage me every step of the way as I grew as a person, wife, and mom. You cheered me on as I built a business out of thin air. You've seen me at my best and at my worst—and you loved me through it all. Your friendship is unmatched, and I am beyond thankful that you accepted my offer to sit at my table that fateful day in college.

A special thank-you to Chris Browning and Bola Sokunbi. Chris, thank you for always believing in what I can do, even when I doubt you at first. Thanks for being there to tell me, "I told you so" when I reach new heights. Bola, thank you for helping me turn the idea of writing a book into a reality. You are generous with your encouragement, time, and kindness. I'm lucky to call you a friend.

To my team at Wiley: Carla, Sheck, and Kelly. Thank you for standing by this book and having the confidence that it can have an impact in the reader's life. Without your support, this book would only live in my mind.

To the Inspired Budget Community and everyone who has welcomed me into their life—thank you. My mission is to inspire you, but in a surprising turn of events, you have inspired me. You have taught me to dream bigger, step out of my comfort zone, and believe in myself more than I ever could have imagined. Thank you for giving me the space to teach, encourage, and motivate you on every step of your money journey.

About the Author

Allison Baggerly is a blogger, author, influencer, speaker, podcaster, and founder of Inspired Budget, which is proudly a Hispanic and women-owned business. A former teacher, Allison blends her talents for teaching with her passion for personal finances to help others learn how to start budgeting and build a life they love.

Allison and her husband paid off over $111,000 of debt on two teachers' salaries while growing their family. During the process, she learned how to take back control of her money, stay consistent with paying off debt, and stop emotional spending once and for all.

Allison has been featured in *Forbes* and *Parents* as a budget expert who gives women a step-by-step process to break free from the grueling paycheck-to-paycheck cycle. Women turn to Allison, and Inspired Budget, for advice and inspiration every single day.

Chapter 1

Finding Your Catalyst

I sat at the kitchen table with my head in my hands. Tears streamed down my face as my husband and I were hit with the reality of how far out of control our finances were. We had just found out we were unexpectedly pregnant a few weeks after getting married. After completing some simple math, we realized we would not be able to afford monthly daycare payments.

My husband and I totaled up exactly how much debt we had: $111,108.29 (not including our mortgage). Our minimum monthly payments totaled over $1,400 each month. I did a double take. Surely we had made a mistake when adding all of our debt into the calculator! For two teachers, this might as well have been a fortune.

What were we going to do? How would we pay for childcare? Don't kids eat a lot? How would we afford groceries? And *oh my goodness don't hospitals cost a fortune?!*

Anxiety and fear clouded my mind. I couldn't think straight. I just wanted to pretend that we didn't have a problem. I wanted to go back to when we thought everything was perfectly fine. I wanted to believe our money wasn't an issue.

That day at the kitchen table in our small apartment sat two twenty-something adults who had no clue how to pull themselves out of the mess they had created. I felt like we were standing at the bottom of a mountain and had no idea how to climb to the top. We didn't have a path to take, a map to follow, or the tools to get there.

That moment was our breaking point, our rock bottom. To be honest, my spending habits were downright embarrassing and completely unhealthy. My husband, the saver in our marriage, let me spend money because he thought it would bring me joy. "Happy wife, happy life" they say! Unfortunately, my temporary happiness from buying stuff I could not actually afford was setting us up for a world of pain and debt. And our previous choices about taking out massive amounts of student loans left these two schoolteachers feeling completely hopeless.

Teachers are underpaid, overworked, and usually have to supplement their income in some way. I almost resigned myself to the idea that I'd always be waiting on my next paycheck and never be able to go on a nice vacation or live in abundance. My immediate thought was that we would forever feel trapped and suffocated by debt and money. I figured we would never have enough. Enough money, enough freedom, enough peace of mind.

But then a little voice in the back of my head whispered something. It said, "What if it doesn't have to be this way? What if two teachers can defy the odds?"

Beginning the Journey

I didn't know *how* we were going to get out of debt, live on less money, and fix the financial situation we found ourselves in. We had *years* of bad spending habits and mindset issues to unpack. But I knew I could figure it out along the way because I was motivated to live a different life than where we found ourselves. My husband, Matt, and I both knew that it would take work to pull ourselves out of crippling debt on two teacher salaries.

I wish I could tell you that we would have made this choice even if we didn't find ourselves pregnant just a few weeks after getting married. In a perfect world, Matt and I would have made this

2

decision because we wanted it for ourselves as a couple. But I can't tell you that because it would be a lie.

We decided to completely change our financial situation because we *had* to do something different. We took this step to get our money under control for our baby to be. The baby that we didn't even know we wanted. The son that caught us off guard, forced us to take a long look at our life, and do something uncomfortable for someone else. We *had* to put him first. He was our motivation. He was our catalyst. Evan, our precious boy, was our driving force to sacrifice in areas of our lives for a period of time so that we could live in abundance for the rest of our life.

Yet as we continued on our financial journey, our catalyst became even greater than just our son. We wanted it not *just* for him and our second son, James. We wanted it for *us*. We wanted to reach financial success, pay off debt, and be a story that could motivate others.

Our journey began out of desperation. Yet as time went on, it turned into a journey that would create a generational shift for our family.

That day while sitting at my hand-me-down kitchen table surrounded by wobbly IKEA kitchen chairs, I wiped my tears away and decided that this was the moment our lives would change. Matt and I jumped with two feet into the unknown world of managing our money. We had zero knowledge of what we were doing (they don't teach this stuff in school), but we knew we could figure it out as we went.

We just had to start.

Matt and I eventually paid off over $111,000 of debt on two teacher salaries. During our almost five-year journey of paying off debt, we made more mistakes than I care to admit. We weren't perfect. We had moments where we wanted to give up. We were faced with unexpected expenses that set us back months at a time. But after a journey that felt like an eternity, we did it!

Matt and I worked together to create a strong foundation for managing our money, and for the rest of our lives we will reap the rewards of building that foundation. I learned how to conquer impulse spending, how to write a budget that *actually* works, and what to do when I trip and fall along the way. We created our own money management system that worked, and it's the one we still use to this day.

The memory of feeling defeated and hitting rock bottom is just that: a *memory*. It's no longer our financial truth.

But I know rock bottom might be your current *reality*. I know you might be struggling just to keep up with your expenses. You might be hurting and feeling defeated because you have more bills than money coming in. Maybe you feel like a failure with your finances or completely out of control with money. The shame and guilt might keep you up at night.

If that's you, please know you don't have to live in this space forever. You can pick yourself up, defeat the odds, and change your finances. You are capable of more than you likely give yourself credit for. It will take work, but I promise you that it will be worth it!

The Catalyst Is Your Motivator for Change

The first step, and arguably the most important step, is to find a catalyst to change your money situation that is so strong, you won't give up along the way.

Managing your money better, paying off debt, and saying no to impulse purchases takes an enormous amount of discipline. It likely takes more discipline than you're used to. We live in a world that tells us to spend more, put purchases on a credit card, and find happiness from *stuff*. Society tells us that we shouldn't have to wait for *anything*. Do you want new furniture? Finance it! Want to trade in your current car? Just roll it into your next car payment! Can't afford that beach vacation? That's what credit cards are for!

Many people lack the patience to save up for large purchases and eventually find themselves buried in debt. It's easy to get caught up in the exhilaration of buying something new just for the thrill of it. This temporary happiness is present for a moment, but when the excitement of a new item wears off, we are left with the same feelings as before.

I say all this from experience. The first time I bought an "adult" car, it was partly out of necessity. I had a baby on the way, and my car at the time was a two-door Chevy Cavalier with a junk title. I didn't feel comfortable driving around with my newborn son in a car that had been totaled before.

I'll never forget taking my new car out for a test drive. It had a sunroof, leather interior, and automatic windows (I had *never* had a car with automatic windows before! Oh, the luxury!). It even had the number one item on my wish list: a CD player. When I test-drove that pre-owned Toyota Camry, I felt on top of the world.

Side note: I realize how lame this sounds as I type it out. However, this was the nicest car I had ever driven, had features my previous car never had, and is my truth—so I'm going to own it!

I remember driving away from the dealership, breathing in the smell of the leather seats, and thinking, "This car has made me *so happy*. I'll never get over this feeling." What I didn't know then that I know now: feelings from material possessions fade. My car brought me *temporary* joy and happiness. To think I would never get over the happiness of a car, just an item in my life, was short-sighted, to say the least. I know that now.

Yet, the world tries to tell us that spending money is the key to happiness. So many people fall for it, myself included. We spend money emotionally to run away from our feelings or provide the thrill we've been missing. It's a constant battle, and one that most people don't even realize they are facing.

Breaking free from what the world tells us we "should do" isn't easy. It takes a great motivator, or as I like to call it, a catalyst for change. **A catalyst is your reason for changing the way you spend and manage your money. It's *the* reason you will sacrifice for a period of time so you can live in abundance the rest of your life.**

Your catalyst will keep you moving forward when others tell you to give up. It will help you stay motivated when you question *why* you are working to become debt free or live on less than you make. It will be your strength when the world tells you that spending money is the key to happiness. It is your north star, guiding light, and ultimate motivator.

Identifying Your Catalyst for Change

When my husband and I started our money journey in 2012, our catalyst was our first son, Evan. His presence was unexpected and turned our world upside down. We had plans for our marriage, but having a child in the first year of marriage wasn't in our plans.

Evan led us to look at our lives, money, and future through an entirely different lens than we had before. We knew that if we wanted to pay off debt, build wealth, and offer our children a certain life, we would have to make sacrifices in the present moment.

How do you determine your own catalyst for change? How do you find a catalyst that will be strong enough to stand up against society and years of money habits that leave you wanting to spend money? How do you find *the* thing that will be stronger than your emotional desire to go into deep debt for the car you've always wanted? How do you find a motivator that will last the length of your journey—especially if you'll be working on changing your finances for years on end like we were?

You might have *no idea* what your catalyst for changing your financial situation should be. It might take you time to determine your own catalyst. You might have to think through your future, goals, and dreams. Journaling and asking yourself hard questions can sometimes help you uncover the catalyst that will carry you through your financial journey. On the other hand, your catalyst might already be staring you in the face and be clear as day.

Sometimes your catalyst is found when you've hit your rock-bottom moments. It reveals itself when you're at the end of your rope, stressed, overwhelmed, and aware that something has to change. It's sitting there next to you when you have your head in your hands, tears streaming down your face, and there's a deep knowing that *you want something different for yourself and your family.*

It's in these rock-bottom moments that our catalyst appears and becomes the driving force for a different life. It becomes *our reason* for picking ourselves back up, dusting ourselves off, and committing to doing something *different* with our money. My family's catalyst revealed itself in our own rock-bottom moment. While this was difficult to realize, it was enough of a driving force to stay committed to our financial journey for years on end. It was strong enough for us to change our money habits, face our financial truth, and prioritize our needs over our wants.

Your catalyst for change might lie in the seemingly small, annoying, and frustrating moments that add up over time. Moments such as having your debit card declined at the grocery store or realizing you've been hit with yet another overdraft fee. Your catalyst might reveal itself to you in the arguments you have with your spouse about money or the feeling of dread as you open the mailbox and see yet another bill you have to pay. Your catalyst could stem from the sleepless nights where you worry about your finances. Or maybe it's the desire to simply take a vacation every year without going into debt. These small moments add up over time to create a catalyst for you: the desire for control and confidence with money.

Your catalyst for change could also be a person. Maybe that person is you (you are a worthy reason to change your finances and manage your money better!). Maybe that person is your child or even a niece or nephew. Your catalyst could even be your parents. I've known people who witnessed their parents stress about money and saw firsthand what happens when you hit retirement with little money saved. The burden fell on the children. While this person loved their parents with all their heart, they wanted a different life than what was modeled for them. Their catalyst was generational change.

Whatever it is, your catalyst must be strong enough to carry you through this journey to managing your money better, living on a budget, and paying off debt even when it becomes an inconvenience. It must be bigger than the desire to succumb to what the world tells you about money. **Your catalyst needs to be in the forefront of your mind and be greater than the frustrations you might face along the way.**

Before you move forward on your financial journey, I want you to determine your catalyst for change. Take a moment to think about *why* you picked up this book. Why do you want to budget better, or start budgeting altogether? What makes you want to become debt free and save money? The ultimate goal is to dig deep enough to find a reason that will hold strong through the temptation to overspend, go into debt, or give up on your money journey. While you'll never be perfect, your catalyst will be the reason why you stand up after you fall, decide to budget even when you don't feel like it, and slowly make changes with your money.

Use the Catalyst for Change Worksheet to help identify your own catalyst for change. You can use the one provided here or download the worksheet from www.inspiredbudget.com/moneymadeeasy.

Catalyst for Change Worksheet

Why do you want to budget better, or start budgeting altogether?	
What could you accomplish or do if you no longer had debt payments?	
What dreams do you have for your future?	
Who do you want to live a different life for? (It could be yourself or a family member.)	
How does your current financial state make you feel?	
If money was not an issue in your life, how would you spend your days? What would you do?	
If money was not an issue in your life, how would you feel?	

Finding Your Catalyst

Real-world Examples

Over the years I've had the joy of hearing from hundreds of people about their driving forces for change. People come to me when they've hit their rock-bottom moments or are fed up with their financial situation. They come to me when they desperately need a catalyst for change. I've helped guide others to find their own driving force for change.

Table 1.1 provides a list of common catalysts that *many people* have set as their motivator to take back control of their money, spending, and debt.

Table 1.1 Common Catalysts for Change

Catalyst	Desired Change
My future family	*Someone wants to have a child but has health concerns that might affect their ability to safely carry a child. They want to become debt free so they can afford adoption or a gestational carrier.*
My current family	*Someone wants to be a stay-at-home mom but can't do that unless they pay off debt and reduce monthly payments.*
Generational wealth	*A person has seen their parents live paycheck to paycheck their entire life and wants to break this cycle for future generations. Their goal is to create wealth for generations to come.*
Rewrite family history	*Someone has experienced how debt and money stress affected their parents. They want to rewrite their family history and have the freedom that becoming debt free offers.*
Myself	*Someone wants to put themselves and their future first. They want to let go of their past money choices. Paying off debt, saving, and investing is a form of healing for this person.*
A job I love	*Someone wants to escape a career that they don't love. They want the freedom to leave their job and know that they are secure financially.*
My child	*Someone wants their son or daughter to see what financial security looks like. They want to be a model for what it means to be financially successful.*

Catalyst	Desired Change
A better life	*Someone wants a better life than what was modeled for them. They want to break free from any harmful money habits not just for their family but for themselves as well!*

No matter what your catalyst may be, hold it close to your heart. It will be *the* driving force that will get you started and keep you motivated as you learn how to manage your money better.

In the beginning, your catalyst will likely be the only thing keeping you focused and moving forward. Yet as time passes on, you'll have to rely less and less on your catalyst to keep you motivated. Instead, you will have developed helpful money habits that make sticking to your plan easier! This simple fact caught me off guard during our journey.

Creating Internal Motivation

When Matt and I first started budgeting, I *hated* the idea of writing a budget. The entire process felt forced, frustrating, and left me feeling deprived. I figured I would only write a budget until we were debt free. I daydreamed about walking into Target, which I lovingly refer to as "The Motherland," and filling my cart to the brim with items I wanted but did not *need*. I would shop until my heart was happy and the trunk of my car was full. No budget would keep me from spending my money how I wanted! I vowed that once we became debt free, I would be done with budgets *forever* (clearly, the joke was on me because now I'm writing a book about budgeting!).

Little did I know that as time went on, I no longer needed to rely on my catalyst to motivate me. Budgeting and managing my money better were no longer simply tasks I completed. It was no longer something I "did" each day, week, or month. Thinking through my spending was no longer something I had to remind myself to do.

In fact, I actually *looked forward* to budgeting each month (*who was I, and what had I done with past Allison?!*).

The idea of writing a budget, tracking my expenses, and making a plan for my money gave me a new confidence and feeling of security I had never had before.

Budgeting and taking control over my finances had become part of my identity. I wasn't just budgeting each month. *I was a budgeter.* I wasn't just checking off boxes on a list to have control over my money. Instead, managing our finances became part of who I was. I looked forward to payday so I could move money to savings, pay off debt, and take one step closer to our money goals. Over time my money habits naturally changed. I no longer had to force myself to think about my money in a better light, it all came more naturally to me.

It was in that moment I realized I no longer needed my catalyst (our children) to motivate me. While they were, and still are, great motivators for living a better life, I have the motivation within me now. It's a part of who I am. **I have the internal motivation to continue handling my money in a positive way instead of relying on an external motivator.**

You'll be able to experience this as well! As time goes on and as you continue to make small decisions each day about your money, you will develop the internal motivation you need to keep going. You will no longer rely on the catalyst that got you started at the beginning. Your money habits and thinking will change. This takes time. It took *years* for me to realize this, but it's an amazing place to be!

Now it's your turn.

Take a moment to think through your catalyst for change. Before you do *anything* to improve your money or financial situation, what is *the* thing that will keep you motivated when you get started? What is the catalyst that will keep you working on your money when you would rather spend it on something that caught your eye? What's the catalyst that will keep you from picking up dinner after a long day at work when you know you have food at home?

Your catalyst for change will be what you turn to when you want to give up, life gets hard, you're hit with an unexpected expense, or you're just *tired* of making adult choices with your money. It's your reason to keep moving forward each and every day. Keep it at the forefront of your mind from this point on.

Action Items

- Take time to think and journal about the following questions to help you define your catalyst for change:
  - Why do you want to budget better, or start budgeting altogether?
  - What could you accomplish or do if you no longer had debt payments?
  - What dreams do you have for your future?
  - Who do you want to live a different life for? It could be yourself or a family member.
  - How does your current financial state make you feel?
  - If money was not an issue in your life, how would you spend your days? What would you do?
  - If money was not an issue in your life, how would you feel?
- Complete the following sentence: My catalyst for changing my financial situation is. . .

Chapter 2

Money Habits and Money Mindset

I slammed the front door with all my might and headed straight for my car. My husband, Matt, and I had just had a huge fight. I was seething with anger, and every part of me needed to escape my apartment, or else I would say something I would later regret. I desperately needed to find space to clear my mind and be in my happy place. It was 10 p.m., and I knew exactly where I was headed: Kohl's.

Kohl's is a department store that carries it all: clothing for all ages, jewelry, handbags, as well as home and bath goods. The reason I chose Kohl's as my safe haven came down to its late hours: Kohl's is open until at least 11 p.m. every night. I opened the heavy glass door and immediately felt a sense of calm and peace rush over me. I shopped at Kohl's until it closed, drove home, and I was no longer angry with my husband. Once again, Kohl's had come through, and I was happy and at peace again. Problem solved.

Simply put, shopping brought me joy. I realize now that this should have been a major red flag for me, but I was blind to it at the time. All I knew was that my blood was boiling at one moment, and the next it was not.

That's all that mattered.

I didn't realize it then, but looking back, I know I was using shopping as an escape mechanism. Instead of facing my fears, anger, or frustrations head on, I shopped.

Instead of allowing myself room to be sad, I shopped.

Instead of having hard conversations and dealing with the problem, I shopped.

Over the years, spending money had turned into a way for me to escape difficult emotions and even celebrate or enhance positive emotions.

This unhealthy pattern solidified itself years earlier when I was in college and had the freedom I had always wanted. I had student loan money burning a hole in my bank account, and I was eager to spend it on anything and everything other than college. With my newfound freedom, my emotional shopping took a turn for the worse. I would spend money not just when I was sad but when I was happy, bored, excited, angry, and every emotion in between.

On the one hand, I used shopping and spending money as a reward. Got a good grade on a test? Get a pedicure! Made the student organization I had applied for? Head to the mall! Worked out four times in a week? Celebrate with a new outfit! Spending money became a default habit for me when I was happy, excited, or proud of my work in college.

On the other hand, I *also* used shopping and spending money to cope with sadness, depression, or any unwanted emotions. Each time I bought a new item this way, I was solidifying a very harmful money belief deep inside me: *I can control my emotions and life by spending money.* Years of childhood experiences related to money and later my adult experiences with money had led to incredibly harmful financial habits and money mindsets that were tough to break.

Money Mindset: What Is It?

Your money mindset is your overall outlook on and beliefs about money. Like it or not, the way you view money today is based on a series of assumptions and deeply held beliefs that you've had for years. Many of these beliefs likely stem from your childhood and early adult years.

But what if you no longer *want* to see money or your finances as you always have? What if you realize now that your current view on money and finances is actually holding you back from the goals you want to reach? What if you want to completely change your outlook on your income, spending, and ability to build wealth? Are you out of luck and stuck with the assumptions you've always had? Gosh, I hope you don't believe that. I know as a matter of fact that you can change those assumptions.

Not enough people challenge their own money mindset, so they miss out on the opportunity to improve their financial situation. In fact, many people aren't fully aware of their money mindset or how it affects both their present and future. Many people might not challenge their money mindset because they didn't realize they *could* challenge and change it. I was one of those people! It took time for me to realize that my mindset, and yours too, is a powerful thing. Better yet, *we are in control of what we believe.*

Challenging your money mindset and creating positive money habits isn't only a starting point. It shapes your entire thought process on important matters from career choices to politics and, of course, money. The way we budget, the way we spend, all the investments we make, and how we respond to money stem from our money mindset. Every aspect of our approach to money has one thing in common—that's our money mindset.

Your money mindset has influenced your current financial situation. It's the same mindset that slowly started forming during childhood and continued into your adult life. To truly understand your money mindset, you must first look back to how money affected your early years.

Your Childhood and Money

A lot of people don't realize this, but the way your parents or guardians talked about finances has likely had a significant impact on your money mindset. It doesn't matter if your parents had a healthy relationship with money or a tumultuous relationship with it. Even if you *never* heard your parents discuss money because it was considered rude or inappropriate to discuss finances in front of children, it still had a major impact on how you view money. Many times, children form a money mindset by simply observing their parents, even when they didn't realize they were watching them.

Children pick up on small conversations or tense moments in the home. They listen to what's going on and ask themselves if everything is okay. As a child, you formed a belief about money that was passed down to you by your parents and even your parent's parents.

The person who witnessed their parents fighting about money on a weekly or monthly basis likely grew up believing money is scarce, causes conflict, and can even tear a family apart.

The person who grew up with a father who controlled the finances and didn't let his partner have a say in how money was spent most likely grew up believing men should handle the money and women should not have a say in the matter.

The person who grew up with parents who worked multiple jobs and sacrificed everything just to keep food on the table likely grew up believing no matter how hard they work, they will always struggle financially.

However, there are times when children make assumptions or form beliefs about their parents and money that aren't necessarily true. Maybe you *thought* your parents divorced over money, but there was a deeper reason for the divorce that you couldn't understand as a child. No matter what, *your perception as a child is your reality.*

Let that sink in for a bit.

As a child if your perception was that money causes arguments or divorce, that was your reality regardless of whether or not money was *actually* the cause of stress in your childhood home. Whatever you perceived as a child was your reality until a parent sat down and explained what was *really* going on in the home. And the perception you have about money from your childhood carries into adulthood.

If you want to move forward and change the way you interact with money, it's important to identify how your childhood influenced your view on money. It can be painful to open up the door to your childhood, especially if it holds trauma that you haven't worked through yet.

But do you want to know the good news about this process? Once you understand what your childhood taught you about money, you have a very important choice to make: you get to decide if you want to *keep* or *let go of* what you learned about money from your childhood. You don't have to stand by what your parents or childhood experiences taught you about money. You *can* change your outlook and mindset about money to serve you better.

However, before you do that, you might have to forgive your parents for *not* teaching you more about how to manage money as an adult. Over the years I've worked with many couples and individuals when it comes to their money. One pattern I've noticed is adults, mainly millennials, are frustrated that their parents and school system didn't teach them about managing money or budgeting earlier on in life. It's easy to think, "I would have been better off financially had my parents taught me basic financial concepts when I was younger."

I've even thought this myself! I remember feeling like I had missed a secret money class in high school where everyone else received valuable life information except me. *Why didn't my counselor sign me up for this class?!*

Money Habits and Money Mindset

However, years after working on my own money mindset, I had a very big realization: our parents (mine, yours, and almost everyone else's) weren't withholding grand information from their children. They weren't planning to push us out into the world and have us figure it all out on our own. Your parents weren't hiding knowledge and hoping you would stumble upon the right books to teach you how to manage money properly.

They, too, were in the midst of learning how to manage their own money.

In fact, learning how to manage your money, write a budget, save, and invest before the Internet was available was a *privilege*. Before the internet, adults only had two ways to learn about finances:

- One option was to have access to a guide. Essentially, this was a person in your life that would have the time, patience, and ability to sit down with you and teach you how to manage money properly. This means your parents had to have access to this person in their family or community. Sometimes this person didn't exist or wasn't available in the community.

- The second option was to know *how* to gather financial information on their own. That means our parents would need to know how to read, check out a library book, and know which books to read in order to learn this information. Just *knowing* how to gather information and consume it in English is also a privilege that many people didn't have.

Learning about money and personal finance was a privilege before the Internet (and it still is to this day). Chances are, if your parents didn't teach you about managing money or the importance of paying credit cards on time, it was likely because they were trying to figure it out while you were a child. How could they teach their children about a concept or way of living that they were still trying to figure out on their own?

20

Money Made Easy

You might be frustrated with your parents for the example they set with money. You might be annoyed that they didn't *talk* about money with you or teach you how to handle your finances properly. But once you realize that your parents did the best they could with what they knew at the time, you can let go of that frustration and replace it with grace instead.

Here's the truth: we are all doing the best we can with what we know at the time. We won't always get it right. We all make mistakes along the way. We won't be perfect. All that matters is that you're willing to own up to your past choices and make the effort to learn and do better for your future. I, for one, am happy to extend this grace to my parents in hopes that my own children will do the same for me one day. Take this moment to also extend grace to yourself. You might be frustrated with your past money choices. Remember this simple fact: you did the best you could with what you knew at the time. The good news is that you're here now learning more about how to manage your money easily. Let go of those past money choices you made, and let's focus on your amazing future!

Thankfully, you and I are not in the same boat our parents were in! We live in a world where we have easy access to the Internet, social media, and content creators that are willing to share their knowledge and guide you along on your own money journey.

The first step to changing your money mindset into one that serves you is by identifying how money in your early years has influenced the way you see and interact with money now.

Take a moment to answer the following questions:

- Did you hear your parents discuss money at home?
- Did your parents fight about money? If so, how did that affect the way you saw money as a child?
- Did money feel scarce in your childhood home?

- Was money a conversation topic you could openly talk about at home?
- What was your most positive money memory from your childhood? Do you think this memory has affected you as an adult?
- What was your most negative money memory from your childhood? Do you think this memory has affected you as an adult?
- Is there a pattern in how you felt about money as a child and how you feel about money now?

Once you've identified how your childhood influenced your money mindset, it's time to decide whether what you learned from your money story in those early years is serving you today.

Do you want to carry the money beliefs that you've held for years?

If the answer is "yes," then great! You're on the right path. If the answer is "no," then that's okay too! You can let go of these beliefs and develop your own set of beliefs from this moment forward.

That's the wonderful part—you have a choice in this!

Scarcity vs. Abundance Money Mindset

I was at recess watching my fourth grade students play one spring day when another teacher walked over to where I was standing. He told me he had heard my husband and I were trying to pay off our student loans. By this point in our journey, I was very vocal about our goals and our mission. My husband and I were fired up and excited to become two debt-free teachers.

This man was a teacher in our school, and so was his wife. They were both about 15 years older than my husband and me. Because

22

Money Made Easy

we *appeared* to have so much in common, he thought it was appropriate to share his own opinion about *our* goals.

"I hear you and Matt are trying to pay off debt, even your student loans," he said with a big smile.

"Yes, we have a big goal we are trying to reach!" I replied.

I'll never forget his next words because they cut so close to home.

"Good luck with that. You'll always have debt because you're just two teachers." He gave a small laugh, put his hands in his pockets, and walked away.

I was shocked.

I couldn't find any words. I stood at the playground speechless, wondering how he knew one of my deepest fears and insecurities.

How did he know what I had once believed to be true? His words mirrored the thoughts I held before we started our debt-free journey. These were the *exact* words I told myself that fateful night while sitting at the kitchen table with my husband. *I'll always have debt because we are just two teachers.*

I believed we would *never* become debt free on two teachers' salaries. I believed we would *never* build wealth as two teachers. I believed we were destined for the paycheck-to-paycheck life because of our jobs.

I sat in silence and shock until a new thought emerged. One that would have never revealed itself years prior.

Just because YOU still have student loans doesn't mean I have to.
Just because YOU are a teacher and have debt doesn't mean that's my future.
Just because this is YOUR reality doesn't make it mine.

That was the first time someone openly questioned our family's personal money choices. It was the first time someone thought they could blatantly force their scarcity mindset about money on me.

Yet it was also the first time I thought, "Just watch me—I know what I'm capable of."

Just because you may not have a high-paying job doesn't mean you can't reach your money goals. You *are* capable of becoming debt free. You are capable of investing, building wealth, and living a different life from the one the world paints for you. It all starts with *one* step in the right direction.

To the fellow teacher who laughed at me that day: You were wrong.

His scarcity mindset was rearing its ugly head that day, and he attempted to force that mindset on me. What he didn't know was that I had already done the work to let go of my scarcity money mindset and create an abundance money mindset. Thank goodness I had done the work on myself or else I may have believed the money lies he was telling me.

A scarcity mindset is the belief that there will never be enough of something. When applied to money, a scarcity mindset can manifest itself in several ways. It leads us to believe money lies that we need to unpack.

Someone with a scarcity money mindset thinks:

- "I'll never make enough money."
- "There is not enough money in the world for me."
- "I'll always struggle financially."
- "I have to buy this item I want now because I'll never be able to afford it in the future."

- "A teacher (even a dual-income household of two teachers) can never become debt free."

An abundance mindset is the complete opposite. When you have this mindset, you believe that there is enough of everything, for everyone.

If you have an abundance money mindset, you think:

- "There's more than enough money in the world for me."
- "I can buy this item later because money will come to me."
- "There will always be enough money to meet my goals."
- "I can become debt free no matter my profession—even if I'm 'just' a teacher."

So how do you replace a scarcity mindset with an abundance mindset when it comes to your money?

It all comes down to identifying the money lies we believe and how we react to our money. Rewriting this thought process will take time. *But doesn't it make sense that this would take time?* You've been thinking one way for a very long time, so naturally it will take time and effort to rewrite those thoughts.

If you've had a scarcity mindset about money, chances are it's been forming for years on end. However, you are the gatekeeper to your mindset. And you can shift your mindset at any time.

Stop Believing Money Lies

It's self-determination, discipline, and the right mental approach to money that drives even the most economically challenged to overcome odds and build wealth that will last generations. Your money mindset can drive you forward or drag you back.

You've had money thoughts and beliefs for years. But if these thoughts are no longer serving you, then it's time to completely rewrite these thoughts. **Your scarcity money thoughts are essentially money lies that you're telling yourself.**

I turned to social media to ask my followers and community to share the money lies they've believed in the past or present. I was amazed to read their responses. Below are just a handful of them:

- *Budgets are limiting. I can't enjoy my life on a budget.*
- *Investing is for rich people.*
- *I don't make a lot of money, so I'll always be broke.*
- *I'll start budgeting when I make more money.*
- *I'm too old to save for retirement. I started too late.*
- *I'm bad with money, so why bother trying to manage it?*
- *I was raised poor, so that is my future.*
- *I'll never save enough for retirement, so I'll have to work forever.*
- *I owe too much to ever get out of debt.*

These money lies are usually based on emotions, past experiences, and our own limited mindset. They are easy to believe because you've likely believed them for years on end, but once you recognize these thoughts as lies, you *can* completely change them! It all comes down to questioning the money thoughts that enter your mind. This practice takes time, and the more you practice, the easier it will become.

When a scarcity money thought, or money lie, enters your mind, ask yourself these five questions:

1. Is this money thought true?

2. How do I feel when I believe this money thought?

3. How do I treat myself when I believe this thought?

4. What if I didn't have this money thought? How would I feel? Would it have an impact on my confidence to handle money?

5. How can I replace this thought with one that serves me better?

For example, years ago I believed the lie that my husband and I would *forever* have student loans. It felt nearly *impossible* to pay them all off. The accruing interest, high minimum payments, and astronomical loan balance were overwhelming. Our student loans alone could have deterred us from the dream of becoming debt free because we had over $80,000 of student loan debt looming over us.

However, I questioned the lie that "I will always have student loans" and learned how to reframe that thought. Below is an example of how I would question and reframe this money lie.

Money Lie: *I will always have student loans.*

1. Is this money thought true? *No. I guess I could pay them off even if it takes me the entire lifetime of my teaching career.*

2. How do I feel when I believe this money thought? *I feel like a failure. I'm angry with myself for taking out so many student loans or choosing a career path that doesn't pay as much. I'm annoyed, saddened, and frustrated with where I've found myself. I feel stuck and I'm disappointed that my past choices are affecting my children.*

3. How do I treat myself when I believe this thought? *I'm filled with shame, and I tell myself that I should have known better.*

I feel dumb and believe everyone else knew something that I didn't know. I'm not kind to my past self when I believe that I'll have student loans forever.

4. What if I didn't have this money thought? How would I feel? Would it have an impact on my confidence to handle money? *If I didn't believe that I'll always have student loans, I would feel more confident. I would feel at peace regardless of whether or not I had student loans. I wouldn't feel like my student loans are such an emotional burden and instead see them as a hurdle to overcome. My student loans would have no weight on how I view myself or my past choices.*

5. How can I replace this thought with one that serves me better? *I won't always have student loans. I can pay them off, and it will be worth the effort I make. My children will see me and my husband work hard to prioritize our money. They will see what it's like to celebrate hard work and reach your goals.*

The first time you question your money lies or scarcity mindset, it will likely feel unnatural. Don't let that deter you! The reason it feels unnatural is because you've never questioned these thoughts before. Instead, you accepted them as fact when they are actually just thoughts based on emotions.

Speaking of emotions, people often feel embarrassed or ashamed when they try to identify things about themselves that they want to change. They feel like they are somehow saying they are bad or did something wrong to end up with these mindsets. You can't let these emotions get in your way. The reality is that you're just human. We all are. Embrace it and be honest when questioning your money lies.

When you're willing to rewrite the money lies that enter your mind, you'll be one step closer to creating a money mindset that brings you joy and abundance. The five questions for addressing money lies were partially inspired by Byron Katie's "The Work," which is a process for identifying what can make you happier in life. If you want to learn more about Katie's "The Work," check out https://thework.com/2017/10/four-liberating-questions/.

How To Change Your Money Mindset

Once you've learned how to question your money lies and replace them with healthier thoughts, you're on the right track! But because I *love* offering more than just one way to reframe your scarcity money thoughts, here are seven helpful tips to help guide your money mindset in the right direction!

1. **Know what you want money for.** *What would you do if $100,000 landed in your lap right now?* This is such a simple question, yet it's difficult to answer if you have the wrong money mindset. You might have a roadblock keeping you from fully understanding the potential of a large sum of money.

   How would you use it?

   The thing that separates people who have money from people who don't is often sometimes as simple as answering this question. The key is in understanding that whatever your answer is, *you don't need $100,000 to start doing it.* Those who have money and build wealth typically have it because they are willing to save first and spend second. They understand that the only way to build wealth is to save and invest a portion of their income.

You can begin today by taking control of the direction your money flows.

In other words, it's time to write a budget and tell your money where to go before it gets away from you.

If you live paycheck to paycheck and watch all of your money go to bills, the first step to changing your money mindset is realizing that you have an obligation to dictate your finances. That goes for everything from debt management to investment strategies. You get a choice when it comes to your money. It's time to take an active role in deciding where it goes.

2. **Dream about your abundance.** Imagine you had more than enough money to live.

What would your dream life look like?

If you always had abundance, what would you do with that financial abundance?

Would you leave the job you hate or start your own business?

Would you book a luxurious vacation every year?

Or maybe you would invest and build your wealth as quickly as possible so that you could retire five years sooner.

Give yourself permission to dream about what abundance would look like for you.

If you had "enough" money for yourself, what would you do each day? What type of clothes would you wear? Which charities would you support? Where would you travel? How would you travel? Would you only fly first class?

Dreaming about the good that money can do in your life can help you transition into an abundance mindset. Sit down with a blank piece of paper and answer these questions. You might feel silly dreaming so big, but what harm can it do? As you're dreaming of abundance, notice which areas of your life are already abundant as well.

3. **Get focused on your budget.** Avoidance is probably the number one reason why people get comfortable with debt and living paycheck to paycheck. Your mindset may have you thinking your situation can't be helped. You may tell yourself that debt is normal or that for whatever reason you can't make enough money. For whatever reason, you are stuck.

If you feel stuck, there are plenty of good reasons why that is! One big reason is that it is entirely too easy to go about your business and never look at your personal finances.

Spending money is easy—too easy.

Most payments are by subscription now, which means you spend more in the long run and have actual ownership of much less. It also means that automated payments and withdrawals can take on a life of their own.

It's easy to adopt the mindset that you can't control your budget. *But you can.* You just have to look at it and start making decisions you've been avoiding for a long time.

Financial language can also be misleading. The financial industry is highly regulated, so you may feel like you need a law degree to understand economics. You don't.

Writing a budget isn't the hardest part of managing your money. Writing a budget involves simple math. The struggle lies in sticking to the budget you wrote. It lies in the fact that we are emotional beings and money is emotional. You will only reach your money goals once you've developed the discipline to say, "No" or "Not now" when it comes to spending.

It comes down to choosing what you're willing to sacrifice now in order to live in abundance later. We will dive into your budget in Chapter 3, "Creating Your Budget," and Chapter 4, "The Secret Behind Successful Budgeting," and I know you'll walk away with an amazing plan for creating a budget you can actually stick to!

4. **Learn more about money and finance.** If you want to live in a world where more money comes to you, then it's time to learn more about money. Just like you would practice Spanish each day if you wanted to learn how to speak Spanish, spend time each day learning about money.

In today's world, there are many ways to learn about personal finance. No matter how you choose to learn, there's an option you'll likely love! By simply reading this book you're already on the right path! The more you learn, the more confident you will become.

Start by finishing this book and then picking up others like it. There are dozens of amazing financial podcasts for free you can listen to, or simply fill your social media feed with people who are willing to teach you about personal finance. As you learn more about managing your finances, you're opening your mind up to develop an abundance mindset.

5. **Avoid negative comparison.** Comparison is a major source behind many people's money mindset. While comparison can be extremely harmful (a negative comparison), and in general you should avoid it, there is one exception: it can also motivate

you to reach for your dreams (a positive comparison). Let's look at a situation where a negative comparison can harm your money mindset.

Imagine that you're sitting on your sofa scrolling through Instagram. You see a friend you knew from high school who is taking yet another family vacation. "How can she afford these seasonal vacations?!" you wonder.

Immediately comparison sets in. Your mind moves to what you are *not* doing: taking vacations. As you sit there looking through her beach pictures, you start listing the reasons why you *can't* take vacations. You're too busy, too broke, and your kids would fight the entire time.

Sound familiar? This simple comparison leaves you feeling defeated and like you don't have enough money or time.

Now let's imagine that you're scrolling past the same exact vacation pictures. This time, you see what your old high school friend has been able to accomplish. Just as negative comparison starts to close in on your mind, you remind yourself that this is just a reminder of what is possible.

You too can have seasonal vacations! You know you can replicate what you're seeing because it's already been done! Instead of feeling defeated, you feel inspired to reach those same goals!

See how comparison can harm or inspire you? The good news is that you can choose how you will respond.

6. **Practice gratitude daily.** The daily practice of gratitude is one of the easiest ways to start your journey toward a positive money mindset. The more we see the things in life that we are

grateful for, the more abundance we recognize in our own life! Each morning (or each night), write down three things you're grateful for. You can jot them down in your phone or use a journal that you keep by your bedside table.

Having trouble finding something you're grateful for? Don't overthink it! Gratitude can come in the smallest things. A warm cup of coffee, pretty weather, and being able to make your mortgage payment easily can all be things to be grateful for.

Practicing gratitude trains your brain to find the good in every day. This helps you develop a positive mindset about money and your finances as well.

7. **Be intentional with your money.** When it comes to money, there's one truth we must accept: we likely can't have everything we want. However, sometimes we find that we are spending money on things we don't *actually* want. In fact, sometimes we are spending hundreds of dollars each month on subscriptions, services, and bills that don't bring us joy.

When you are intentional with the money you are spending, you're willing to spend money on what's most important to you and your family. If travel is important, then save several hundred dollars each month for your upcoming trip. Don't have room in your budget for those savings? That's okay! It's time to cut out what isn't important for you.

Think of it this way: *spend money on what matters most, and cut out the rest.*

For you, this might look like canceling Spotify, a few more subscriptions, and switching from a major cell phone carrier to a less expensive company.

When you're intentional about how you're spending the money you earn, you might be surprised to learn that you actually do have enough!

Your Money Mindset Matters

If you change the way you look at money today, it will change your future! One setback many of us reach is regret over not doing enough when we were younger. That regret feels like a missed opportunity that will plague us forever. However, what it should do is wake us up to today.

If we don't seize upon our current opportunities to invest in ourselves and our future, we have learned nothing from past mistakes. We will continue to make them today. The biggest mistake would be to give up and always feel like you missed the boat. **It's never too late to change your money mindset and start building your wealth with purpose and intentionality.**

Your money mindset matters—today, tomorrow, and years from now. Start *now* and work to change your outlook on money.

Money Habits: What Are They?

Your money habits are a direct result of your money mindset. Your money mindset helps build and create your money habits. They are the habits you have that surround your personal finances. You can have both harmful and helpful money habits. If you have a scarcity money mindset, you will likely have harmful money habits. As you work on creating an abundance or healthy money mindset, your money habits will follow.

A harmful money habit is a money habit that does not serve you or your future. It often leads to overspending or signing up for future debt payments. I like to think of these as your financial red flags. These habits will *not* get you where you want to be financially.

For instance, my first year out of college, I received a tax refund for $800. I couldn't believe it! $800 was *all mine*. I only had $200 in savings at the time, and the *wise* choice would have been to save my entire refund (or at least most of it). However, I spent my entire tax refund plus some to book a cruise with one of my best friends.

I remember thinking, "I don't know when I'll have this money again, so I better use it now!" My harmful money habit was immediately spending windfalls of money because I didn't know if, or when, more money would come my way.

You might not even recognize the harmful money habits you are currently facing in your life. We tend to be blind to these habits because we are so close to them. They are usually based on emotions that cause us to justify habits that might harm us and our money goals. Thankfully, you *can* replace your harmful money habits with helpful money habits.

A helpful money habit is a habit that helps you reach your financial goals. It's a habit that supports your financial progress and can have a lasting effect on your money. One example of a helpful money habit is tracking your spending so you can see *exactly* where your money is going. I started tracking my spending many years ago. A few times each week I log every expense and transaction on a spreadsheet. This allows me to see our spending in action and identify where we tend to overspend. Because I track our spending, I am able to find patterns in our spending. If I'm unhappy with the patterns I find, my husband and I come up with a plan to reach our goals. The simple money habit of tracking our spending helps us know our money inside and out so we can take the next steps to reaching our money goals.

How to Identify Harmful Money Habits

When I was in college, I dated a guy that I was absolutely infatuated with. He *seemed* perfect in every single way. The only problem? He was throwing me three red flags that I was completely blind to.

Red flag #1: I was so excited for him to meet my friends and family, yet he *never* wanted to introduce me to his friends or family. In fact, when his family came into town he *insisted* that I stay away. Plus, if we happened to run into some of his friends that I didn't know, he wouldn't introduce me to them at all.

Red flag #2: Our relationship was hot and cold. We were constantly breaking up and getting back together. It was *awful*. I spent months crying over this guy and was blind to the fact that this type of relationship was incredibly unhealthy.

Red flag #3: The *biggest* red flag of all was that my friends and family couldn't stand him. My mom told me that she didn't trust him, and my two best friends encouraged me to dump him and spend time focusing on myself. I continued to defend him even though the three people I trusted most at the time were all telling me how terrible he was.

Sadly, I was blind to all three red flags. Why? *Because I was too close to the situation.* I was deeply involved, and my emotions were wrapped up in the relationship. I couldn't see him for what he *really* was: a man-child who was absolutely terrible for me.

Why am I sharing this embarrassing relationship that I wish I could completely forget? Because the *same* thing happens with our money. We are sometimes *blind* to our own red flags when it comes to our finances. Our emotions are wrapped up in our money and sometimes drive our decisions in the wrong direction. We defend our actions, ignore the well-meaning advice of others, and assume we know best. It's not until we hit rock bottom and see all of life's distractions, impulse buys, and our own harmful money habits for what they really are: red flags we couldn't see.

You might have harmful money habits that have gone unnoticed for years on end because you're too close to the situation to recognize these habits clearly.

The first step to replacing these harmful money habits with helpful habits is to recognize them. We have to remove the blinders, put our emotions aside for a moment, and see the red flags for what they truly are: a threat to our financial health.

But how do you recognize these habits when you've been blind to them for so long?

Sometimes we need a little guidance to help us unearth what we've ignored for years. You can start by doing these three things:

1. Face your financial truth;

2. Find patterns in your spending; and

3. Confide in someone.

Face Your Financial Truth

To help you identify your harmful money habits, you must start with your financial truth. These are the numbers and figures of your finances. The facts don't lie and will highlight your money habits. Fill out the My Money Truth Worksheet to face your financial truth. You can also download a free printable version of this chart at www.inspiredbudget.com/moneymadeeasy. It might take a little work to gather all the information, but I promise it will open your eyes to your financial truth.

My Money Truth Worksheet

Checking Account Balance	Savings Account Balance
If you have several checking accounts, you can either list them separately or add them all together.	*If you have several savings accounts, you can either list them separately or add them all together.*
Total Debt (not including mortgage)	Retirement Savings
Be sure to include any debt in collections as well.	*If you are not sure how much you have saved, reach out to your HR department, and they can help you find the information.*

Now that you've completed this table, you are ready to face your financial truth. Don't let these numbers intimidate or scare you. Yes, your total debt might be higher than you thought it would be. Sure, you might not have as much money saved for retirement as you had hoped. But the only way to move forward is to know your starting point. This is your starting point.

- Look at these numbers, and ask yourself how they make you feel. Are you proud of where you stand financially?
- Is there anything you'd like to change?
- Which of these facts pull on your emotions the most, in either a negative or positive way?

Money Habits and Money Mindset

These numbers can reveal money habits that you might not have recognized before. For instance, if you have high credit card payments, you might realize that you tend to rely on your credit card to cover your expenses when you've run out of money. This cycle of using credit keeps you in debt and using your credit card as a crutch.

Find Patterns in Your Spending

When I was a sophomore in college, I found myself sitting on the floor of my childhood home with my head in my hands, crying. My mom was next to me with a calculator in one hand and my bank statements in another. *I had absolutely no money in my checking account—and what's worse is that I had no idea I was broke.*

My loving mother said she would give me money under *one* condition: I faced my spending habits.

We totaled up how much money I was spending from the past two months on eating out, clothes, pedicures, drinks, and more. I remember being in complete shock when I saw just where my money was going.

I couldn't ignore it anymore: **I had a spending problem.**

That day was one of my most shameful moments. I felt like I was failing at adulting and that I had done everything wrong. However, there was a silver lining: I was now *aware* of my habits. I couldn't ignore the patterns anymore—I had to face my truth and do something to change how I was handling and spending money.

Simply reviewing your spending can open your eyes to financial habits you might be blind to. Start by printing off your last two months bank statements. Get a highlighter and highlight every time you spent money on restaurants. Then, add that number up to see what you spent over two months on eating out.

Grab a different color highlighter and highlight every time you spent money at the grocery store. It's easy to overspend at the grocery store and justify the cost. Add up the transactions to see how much you spent on groceries over the past two months. The number might shock you!

Do the same for other areas of your spending such as clothing, entertainment, online shopping, and so on. Then, find an area that you are determined to improve. Maybe you want to spend less on groceries, so you decide to start meal planning. Sometimes the simple act of knowing where your money is going is enough of a catalyst for change.

Confide in Someone

As someone who struggles with impulse spending, I find it easy to justify unnecessary purchases. I can *always* come up with a valid reason for spending money. It's like a superpower but can ultimately lead to crippling debt. Because of this superpower, it's hard for me to identify when I am overspending at times. That's why I have to lean on my husband, Matt, to help hold me accountable. He helps me recognize when I've fallen into the cycle of overspending.

People who love us and know us well can sometimes see our harmful money habits before we can. This is true in my marriage. My husband can see my impulse spending kick in and the desire to keep up with others before it even registers for me. There are times I have to ask him for help creating more boundaries with our money. Otherwise, I would spend it all, and we'd have nothing left for savings and investments.

To help you identify your own money habits, turn to someone you know and trust. Ask them if they have seen or can identify any of your harmful money habits. Keep an open mind to what they are saying, and realize that just because you have had these habits in the past doesn't mean they define who you are as a person. You *can* replace your harmful money habits with healthy habits once you've identified what they are.

Replacing Your Money Habits

You're here because you have money goals you want to reach in your life. I applaud you for that! To reach these goals, you'll have to create helpful money habits that will allow you to get there.

As you can see in Figure 2.1, now that you've identified your money mindset and harmful money habits, it's time to put helpful money habits in place.

Habits take time to implement, but the more often you practice these habits, the more likely they will become second nature. It's important to have two types of helpful money habits in place:

1. Healthy habits to combat your harmful money habits; and

2. Habits that keep you on track to reach your goals.

Chances are you have a handful of harmful money habits that have become second nature to you. It's easy to fall back into these habits because they have been a part of who you are for so long. This is why it is important to have helpful money habits to combat your harmful money habits.

For example, if you tend to online shop in the evening when you're bored, what helpful habit can you put in place to curb that

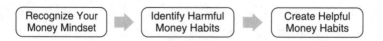

Figure 2.1

desire? Maybe instead of online shopping, you find a good book to read. Or instead of online shopping, you spend that time updating your budget and spending trackers. It's important to replace these harmful habits with ones that will help you reach your goals. Choose a few activities or things you can do when you have the urge to online shop.

It's also important to develop money habits that will help you reach your money goals over time. One example is using cash envelopes for areas where you tend to overspend. I personally find it *very* easy to overspend at the grocery store and while eating out. To help me stay on track with our budget, I use cash for our grocery shopping and restaurant spending. Essentially, I pull enough cash out of the bank on payday for these two categories. I place the cash I need for groceries in an envelope labeled "groceries." I take this envelope with me to the grocery store because it helps keep me on track with my spending. I know that I cannot go overboard with grocery shopping because I can only spend what I have in the envelope.

Using cash envelopes has helped me personally create healthy money habits such as developing patience when shopping, planning ahead before spending, and staying on track in areas where I tend to go overboard.

Take time to think through helpful money habits you can implement in your own life. Some examples of helpful money habits you can try include:

- Track your expenses every day or each week;
- Wait three days before buying an item online;
- Meal plan to help keep grocery costs down;
- Pay your bills early to avoid late fees;

- Look over your budget weekly;
- Call a friend when you're tempted to impulse spend;
- Avoid stores where you're tempted to overspend;
- Order your groceries online so you can track how much you're spending; and
- Talk with your partner weekly about your finances.

Don't overdo it when it comes to creating helpful money habits. If you try to adopt too many habits at once, you'll become over-whelmed and will likely give up along the way.

Instead, choose one or two habits that you would like to imple-ment in your life for two to three months. Once those habits have become second nature, add another helpful money habit to your life.

Time: The Ultimate Gift

Creating money habits that will help you reach your goals will take time. I'm guessing you've spent years enforcing and practicing harm-ful money habits. It's unrealistic to think that you will develop new habits overnight. This isn't a race.

The ultimate goal isn't to create change for just a few months or a year. The goal is to create financial change that will last a lifetime. Remember this fact in the chapters to come.

Action Items

- Answer the following questions about your childhood and money:
  - Did you hear your parents discuss money at home?
  - Did your parents fight about money? If so, how did that affect the way you saw money as a child?

- Did money feel scarce in your childhood home?

- Was money a conversation topic you could openly talk about at home?

- What was your most positive money memory from your childhood? Do you think this memory has influenced you as an adult?

- What was your most negative money memory from your childhood? Do you think this memory has influenced you as an adult?

- Do you see a pattern in how you felt about money as a child versus how you feel about money as an adult?

- Make a list of the money lies you've believed. Question and challenge the lies to help you develop an abundance money mindset.

- Journal and dream about what abundance would look like in your life.

- Identify three to five harmful money habits in your life. Use the following strategies to recognize them:

  - Complete the My Money Truth Worksheet;

  - Categorize your past spending; and

  - Confide in someone.

- List two or three helpful money habits that you want to implement in your life.

Chapter 3

Creating Your Budget

I wanted to scream.

The thought *"Why do I even bother trying"* played on repeat in my mind. With clenched fists and anger welling up inside me, I realized that Matt and I weren't as prepared to handle our money as I had originally thought.

Let's rewind to one week prior. Matt and I had spent an afternoon listing out our expenses and writing what we thought was the *perfect* budget. It was wonderful on paper. This budget covered all our needs and allowed us to set aside money for our upcoming hospital bills when our son Evan arrived.

We were both beaming with pride at the budget we had created! I was excited and admittedly a little nervous to start the process of budgeting and paying off debt.

For years Matt and I had absolutely *no* control over our money. I was determined for this to be *the moment* that everything changed. I imagined everything falling into place beautifully. Our hopes were high, and we fully believed that what we put down on paper would magically happen. It was almost as if we believed that writing our budget was the *hardest* part. What could possibly go wrong?

Well, the joke was on us because just seven days later it was completely ruined.

How on earth did we miss so many expenses?
How did we mess it up so much?

We were over budget in several areas and had completely for-
gotten to include several expenses in our budget.

Realization set in. We didn't know how to write a budget we
could *actually* stick to. I was angry enough that I wanted to give up
on budgeting altogether and throw my budget in the trash. Part of
me even started to believe it would always be this way.

Heck, I was ready to head to my nearest Target, buy a grande
Starbucks latte, and just *shop*. I knew that I would immediately
feel better if I started filling that glorious red cart with items that
made me *happy*.

But a small voice in my head told me that this entire budgeting journey and managing our money better came with a learning
curve (and that a Target shopping trip wouldn't *actually* help). Why
did I automatically assume we would get it right the first time? Just
like a child learning to ride a bike for the first time, there would be
bumps and bruises along the way. We would fall down and have to
pick ourselves back up.

Even though every part of me wanted to give up that day,
I knew we had goals. We had a vision for our life, and there was
only one way to reach those dreams: we would have to build a
strong financial foundation. This foundation began with our budget.
We wanted our budget to help us live on less, stop the paycheck-to-
paycheck cycle, pay off debt, and save for retirement.

It took several attempts for us to realize that our first few budgets
were completely unrealistic. Instead of writing a budget that repre-
sented our real life, we were writing a budget that looked like a life
we didn't even *want* to live! It took us time to learn more about our
spending habits, where our money was going, and how to write a
budget that would work for us.

If you're struggling with writing a budget, you might feel confused, overwhelmed, and lost. Listen up—you are not alone. Writing a budget can feel daunting when you are trying to take back control of your finances.

You already know that a budget can help you reach your money goals. It is the tool that will be the guiding force when it comes to your money. It paves the way for what you will accomplish financially, whether that's comfortably making ends meet each month, paying off loans and credit cards, or enjoying family vacations at the beach. I even like to think of it as the GPS that helps me reach my destination.

Writing a budget doesn't have to be complicated, but it's important to find a system that works for *you*. Your budget and plan won't look like everyone else's—indeed, why should it? You are your own unique person, and your family has specific needs. The goal isn't to create a cookie-cutter budget that someone else could pick up and use. **The goal is to create a budget that is specific and unique to your life. Then, and only then, will you be able to write a budget that you can *actually* stick to.**

What Is a Budget?

Can I make a confession?

I used to think that budgets were *terrible*. Even the word "budget" sounded like a punishment. I likened it to a timeout for my money and fun. Mostly, I viewed a budget as a limit on my life. In my eyes it was something that would hold me back from spending money on what I wanted. I was sure that a budget would keep me from enjoying life.

Many people view their budget the same way I did. Why? It's because we fail to think about what a budget can offer us. Instead, we only focus on what a budget will *take away* from our lives.

Instead of hating the word "budget" like I did, I want you to think of it this way: **a budget is simply your spending plan or road map for your money.**

Did you ever go on a road trip as a kid and your parents would pull out a paper map to determine the best way to make it to your destination? This was before smartphones were available, and people didn't have access to GPS. Every car contained them: intricately folded maps that were practically impossible to refold correctly. (Second confession: I still have a map in my car because you never know when you'll need one.)

Before embarking on a family road trip, my dad would spread out a paper map across the kitchen table. He would hover over the map with one important mission: determine the *best* (and quickest) way to make it to our end destination. Without the map, he wouldn't know where to go. While there were many routes he could take to reach our destination, my dad's mission was to pick the *best* route.

Your budget is your map, but for your money. It's your opportunity to pick the *best* route to reach your destination, or money goals. Your budget is simply a plan. It doesn't have to be limiting unless you want it to be. Your budget can include as much, or as little, as you'd like.

Do you want to enjoy your favorite latte every Friday morning at your local coffee shop? Perfect! Put it in your budget. Do you want to plan a girls' trip every summer with some of your best friends? I do! Add it to your budget.

Your budget gives you the opportunity to be intentional with your money. It allows you to decide what you *want* to spend money on. It gives you the freedom to prioritize what you value most. Without a budget, many people don't take the time or energy to think about how they want to spend their money. Instead, they are stuck in a cycle of spending when the opportunity arises. Instead of being proactive with their money, they are reactive.

Writing a Budget

Your budget is your money plan. The best part about your budget is that you get to choose where you spend your money. Before we dive into *how* to make those choices, it's important to know how often you'll write a budget.

Step 1: Budget per Paycheck

The first step to writing a budget is to determine *how often* you'll need to write a budget. Many people assume that the best way to budget is to create a budget for each month, starting on the first day of the month until the last day of the month. While this might seem like the obvious solution, this is actually *not* the best way to write a budget.

Instead, it's *much* easier to write a budget for each pay period or paycheck.

When my husband and I first started to budget, we were paid on the 25th of every month. Our budget lasted us from payday, the 25th of one month, until the day before our next payday, the 24th of the next month.

If you are paid monthly, it makes sense to write your budget for the entire month starting from the beginning of one payday until the day before your next payday.

Budgeting for each paycheck or pay period makes budgeting so much easier. If you are paid weekly, you'll want to write a budget each week. If you're paid biweekly, then make a new budget every other week. If you're paid monthly, you'll only have to write one budget a month.

If you have a spouse or partner, you might have to budget differently based on when they are paid. One tip is to lump your paydays that are near each other together to create one combined pay period.

For instance, these days I am paid monthly on the last day of the month, but my husband is paid on the 15th and 25th of every month. We currently write a budget based on his paycheck schedule, but we make sure to pay a majority of our bills right after I am paid. Because we have more money coming into our checking account during the two-week period that we are both paid, it makes sense to pay most of our bills during that time.

As a visual person, I personally love using calendars to see our budget and pay periods "in action." Figure 3.1 shows what our budget for each paycheck looks like on a calendar.

Sunday	Monday	Tuesday	Wednesday	Thursday	Friday	Saturday
	25 Matt Payday Budget #1 →	26	27	28	29	30
31 Allison Payday	1	2	3	4	5	6
7	8	9	10	11	12	13
14 → Budget #1 Ends	15 Matt Payday → Budget #2	16	17	18	19	20
21	22	23	24 → Budget #2 Ends	25 Matt Payday Budget #3	26	27
28	29	30 Allison Payday				

Figure 3.1

You can see that we write two budgets each month. Our first budget starts at the end of the month and lasts us until the 14th of the next month. Then, we have a smaller budget period that lasts us from the 15th until we are paid again. As I mentioned earlier, because our first budget contains both my paycheck and my husband's paycheck, we try to pay most of our bills during the first two weeks of each month.

No matter how you decide to budget, just know that it might take time to find the best schedule for you. Be patient, and know that the more consistent you are with writing your budget, the easier it will become.

Each budget should include three types of expenses: fixed expenses, variable expenses, and debt/savings.

Step 2: List Out Your Income and Fixed Expenses

Once you know when you're paid and how often you'll budget, the next step is to list out your income and fixed expenses on the same calendar.

If you aren't sure how much you're paid each month, then go back through your bank statements or request a copy of your paystub from HR. If your income varies, or fluctuates from one paycheck to the next, don't worry. We will cover that situation in a bit.

Before you write a budget, it's important to know:

1. How many bills you have;

2. How much each bill or expense costs; and

3. When each bill or expense is due.

I personally like to list my expenses on a Bill Payment Log like the one below:

Bill Payment Log

Bill Name	Due Date	Amount Due
Total		$

Fill out the Bill Payment Log above or go to www.inspiredbudget .com/moneymadeeasy to download your own copy of this Bill Payment Log.

Fixed expenses include bills that remain the same from month to month. You can expect to pay the same amount on these bills or expenses every single month. Some examples of fixed expenses that you might want to include in your budget are:

- Mortgage/rent;
- Life insurance;
- Car insurance;
- Dental insurance;
- Daycare/childcare;
- Prescriptions;
- Gym membership;
- Cable;
- Internet;
- Streaming services (Hulu, Netflix, Spotify, etc.); and
- Cell phone.

If you're having trouble remembering all of your bills on the spot, don't worry. Print off your bank statement for both your checking account and credit cards. Read through every transaction, and highlight any recurring bill you have to pay monthly, quarterly, or yearly. Now you'll know *exactly* how many bills you have and when they are due.

Because I'm a visual person, as I mentioned earlier, I love adding my bills to my calendar as well as my bill payment tracker. A calendar is a perfect place to list your bills because you can write them down on their due dates.

Figure 3.2 shows an example of how I would add my recurring bills directly to my calendar.

Sunday	Monday	Tuesday	Wednesday	Thursday	Friday	Saturday
	25 Matt Payday	26	27	28	29	30
31 Allison Payday	1 Mortgage* Car Insurance*	2	3 Life Insurance*	4 Cell Phones* Internet*	5	6
7	8 Netflix* Hulu*	9 Water*	10	11	12	13
14	15 Matt Payday	16	17	18	19	20
21	22 Electricity* Gas(Home)*	23 Charity*	24	25 Matt Payday Budget #3	26 529 College Fund*	27
28	29	30 Allison Payday				
* = Bills on auto draft						

Figure 3.2

It's easy to add a special symbol (e.g. a star) next to the bills that will be automatically drafted from your bank account each month. This way you know which bills you will need to pay manually. Once each bill has left your checking account, add a checkmark next to the bill's name or cross it out completely to show that it's been paid.

Step 3: Budget for Variable Expenses

Once you've included your fixed expenses in your budget, it's time to estimate your variable expenses for each pay period.

Variable expenses include bills or expenses that will change from month to month. The amount due or the amount you spend won't necessarily stay the same every month. The costs of these bills typically vary based on your own personal choices.

Variable expenses tend to be the place where most people get stuck, go over budget, or decide they aren't cut out for this entire budgeting process. For instance, you might budget a different amount for groceries from one paycheck to the next. Your water bill might fluctuate from summer to the winter. These expenses won't be fixed; instead, they vary throughout the year.

Below are examples of variable expenses that you might want to include in your budget:

- Electricity;
- Gas for your home;
- Water;
- Gas for your car;
- Groceries;
- Restaurants;
- School lunches;
- Pocket money;
- Clothing/dry cleaning;
- Gifts;
- Family fun money;
- Personal care (clothing, haircuts, beauty products); and
- Miscellaneous home items (toilet paper, paper towels, trash bags, cleaning supplies).

When you're deciding which variable expenses to include in your budget, think about your life and how you realistically spend money. If you go out to dinner three times each week, estimate how much you'll spend on restaurants and add that to your budget. The goal is to write a budget that truly matches your spending and your life.

It's also okay if you include miscellaneous home items with your grocery budget. This is exactly what our family does. We purchase household items at the grocery store, so we combine these two categories to make everything simpler. The joy of budgeting is that there is flexibility in *how* you budget.

To help make budgeting for variable expenses easy, go back through your last two or three months' bank statements. Look at what you tend to spend money on. Of course, you'll be budgeting for food, gas, and extra spending. Is there any other place where you are spending money? If so, be sure to include that in your budget as well.

Step 4: Budget for Debt Payments and Savings

Don't forget to include debt payments and savings goals in your budget.

Debt payments include any payments you have for student loans, personal loans, credit cards, car loans, or any other loans.

Likewise, if you're saving for a future vacation, back-to-school shopping, or Christmas, then you'll want to add these savings categories to your budget as well.

Below are a few examples of debts or savings categories that you might want to include in your budget:

- Car payments;
- Student loan payments;
- Credit card payments;
- Personal loans;
- Holiday savings;

- Vacation savings;

- Birthday savings; and

- Emergency fund savings.

Start by listing out the minimum payments for each debt you have. This will give you a good starting point for what your budget should look like as you pay off debt. Then, decide how much money you want to save. This number might need to be adjusted after you add up all your expenses.

Step 5: Put It All Together

Once you know *when* you'll be budgeting and *what* you'll include in your budget, it's time to put it all together. Download your own Budget Page at www.inspiredbudget.com/moneymadeeasy. Be sure to save it to your computer so you can print it every time you budget.

Add your fixed expenses, variable expenses, debt payments, and savings to your Budget Page. **Your goal is to live on less than you make:**

Budget Page

Income	Amount
Income Total	

Fixed Expenses	Amount
Total #1	

Debts and Savings	Amount
Total #2	

Variable Expenses	Amount
Total #3	

	Amount
Net Income	
Total 1 + 2 + 3	
Difference	

To help you understand and *see* budgeting in action, here's a sample budget. The following example shows a real monthly budget for a couple who shared it with me. She is a teacher and has a side hustle where she tutors online over the weekend. He is a logistics manager, and they have one child in daycare. Their budget below can give you an idea of how one couple allocates money to all their expenses, savings, and living:

Budget Page Example

Income	Amount
Teacher	$3,500.00
Logistics manager	$4,000.00
Side hustle (extra job)	$400.00
Income Total	**$7,900.00**

Fixed Expenses	Amount
Rent	$1,900.00
Internet	$62.54
Cell phones	$172.96
Car insurance	$152.28
Childcare/day care	$1,320.00
Doctor visits	$185.00
Subscriptions	$35.00
Charity	$200.00
Total #1	**$4,027.78**

Debts and Savings	Amount
Car payment	$396.72
Student loan #1	$315.25
Student loan #2	$394.75
Christmas savings	$100.00
Retirement (Roth IRA)	$200.00
Total #2	**$1,406.72**

Variable Expenses	Amount
Water + trash	$145.00
Electricity	$220.45
Groceries	$800.00
Restaurants	$250.00
Gas (cars)	$200.00
Personal spending	$200.00
Kid's expenses	$100.00
Buffer	$150.00
Total #3	**$2,065.45**

Net Income	$7,900.00
Total 1 + 2 + 3	$7,499.95
Difference	$400.05

This couple has an extra $400.05 leftover each month. They could easily make their budget a zero-based budget by sending this extra money to another area in their budget.

A zero-based budget is a budget where every penny is accounted for. Your total income minus your total expenses equals zero.

Zero-based Budget:
Income – (Expenses + Savings) = $0

To make this a zero-based budget, the couple would need to take the difference of $400.05 and allocate it to another area in their life. They could choose to allocate this extra money to one of their money goals. If they wanted to pay off debt, they could make an extra $400.05 debt payment. If they wanted to increase their emergency fund, they could send the full amount straight to savings.

When you have money left over after you list out your expenses, you have choices when it comes to your money—*and isn't that what you want?* **Choices offer you the ability to focus and prioritize your goals instead of living paycheck to paycheck each month.**

Budgeting on a Variable Income

If your income varies, or isn't the same each paycheck, budgeting can seem *impossible*. In fact, you might long for a steady income like others have. However, just because you don't receive a consistent income doesn't mean you can't have one.

As a small business owner, my income used to change from month to month. When I first started paying myself from my business, I would become very anxious as payday approached. I never knew how much I would end up being able to pay myself because some months I made a lot of money while other months I didn't make enough to cover my portion of our take-home pay. It was very frustrating.

After spending far too many months detesting the ups and downs of a variable income, I decided that I would create my *own* consistent income. If your income varies and you long for a consistent income like others', this method will work for you.

Here's exactly how to budget on a variable income:

Let's say you make between $300 and $700 each paycheck. Your income varies, but it's typically within that range. (Let's also assume your average income is at least $500.)

Step 1: Determine *how much money* you need to cover your expenses during that pay period. For our example, let's keep things simple and assume you need $500 to cover your bills and expenses during that paycheck period.

Step 2: Open a savings account connected to your checking account. Name it "Income Bucket." This is the money that you will use to supplement any paychecks where you make less than you need to cover your expenses.

For paycheck number 1, you earn $700. Instead of keeping all $700, pay yourself $500 to cover your expenses and set aside $200 into your Income Bucket. (See Figure 3.3.)

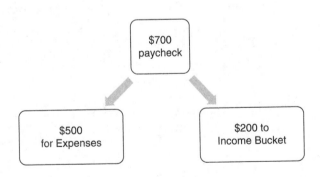

Figure 3.3

Creating Your Budget

For paycheck number 2, you earn $400. This isn't enough money to cover your expenses for that pay period! Instead of stressing and using a credit card to cover your costs, use the $400 you were paid and then pull $100 out of your income bucket to supplement your paycheck. (See Figure 3.4.)

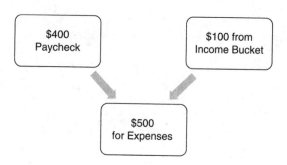

Figure 3.4

Step 3: Every time you earn more money than you need to cover your expenses, or $500 for our example, you will save the extra money in your Income Bucket. Every time you make less than $500, you will supplement the difference from your income bucket. (See Figure 3.5.)

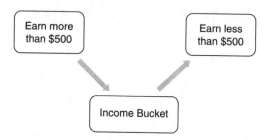

Figure 3.5

As long as you continue to save money in your income bucket, you should have enough money to cover the times you don't make as much as you had hoped.

Want to know the best part about this system?

You are now budgeting off a *consistent* income, which instantly makes budgeting easier! All you have to do is determine how much you need to pay yourself each pay period so you can set up your own Income Bucket system!

Common Budget Percentages

Have you ever faced a problem in your life where you were standing at a fork in the road? Maybe you had a tough decision to make about a friend or a spouse. You're standing there asking for someone to just give you the exact steps to take. "Just lay it all out for me!" you shout.

Unfortunately, I've come to learn that in life we aren't always given a checklist that lays out the next step to take (trust me, I wish I could get my hands on one). There aren't always step-by-step instructions for how to fix a problem.

However, budgeting *can* be just that simple. Sure, dealing with money can be overwhelming. Lots of questions arise. But if you need a plan or checklist to know whether you're doing this whole budgeting thing right, then the 50-30-20 budget might be for you.

The 50-30-20 budget gives you an idea of how much you should be spending on each category of your budget based on how much money you bring home each month. (See Figure 3.6.) It's rather simple. **The 50-30-20 budget instructs you to spend 50% of your take-home pay on your needs, 30% on your wants, and 20% on savings/debt.**

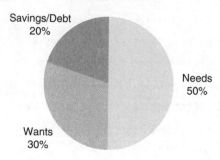

50-30-20 BUDGET

Figure 3.6

50%—Needs

When following the 50-30-20 budget, set aside half your income to cover your basic needs. This includes rent/mortgage, utilities, health insurance, car payment, gas, and groceries. For instance, if you bring home $4,000 each month, you'll want to budget $2,000 for your needs.

Below is a list of expenses that would fall under the needs column.

- Groceries;
- Housing;
- Utilities;
- Health insurance;
- Life insurance;
- Gas;
- Clothing; and
- Childcare.

30%—Wants

Now that your needs are taken care of, set aside 30% of your take-home pay for wants. It's easy to confuse wants and needs at times. For instance, if you're on your way home from work and decide to pick up pizza for dinner because the last thing you want to do is spend time in your kitchen cooking, you *want* the convenience that pizza offers. You don't *need* to pick up pizza. You're more likely to fall off budget or get off track when you overspend in your wants category.

Below is a list of purchases or expenses that would be considered wants.

- Restaurants;
- Dining out;
- Hobbies;
- Pocket money;
- Home décor and furniture;
- Extracurricular activities;
- Travel; and
- Monthly subscriptions.

20%—Savings and Debt

In the 50-30-20 budget, the last 20% of your monthly take-home pay should be allocated to savings or debt. If your goal is to increase your emergency fund, then you can set aside the remaining money from your budget to savings. If you are working to pay off debt, then this money can all go toward debt payments. If you want to save *and* pay off debt, then simply balance the 20% between the two.

The following expenses fall under the 20% category:

- Debt payments;
- Retirement and investments;
- College fund; and
- Emergency fund.

Where Does Charity Fit In?

You might have noticed that charity or giving wasn't listed in any of the categories above. If giving is important to you, then feel free to alter your budget percentages as needed. If you want to give 5% of your income, you could lower your needs budget to only 45%. The joy of this budget is that you can easily edit it to fit your life.

As you budget more often, you won't have to rely on the 50-30-20 budget. It's meant for people who want spending guidelines to follow. It helps you look at your expenses and determine if you're overspending in a certain category. As you continue to work on your budget and finances, you should be able to make your budget unique to you and your family.

Your budget might not match these rules perfectly, and that's okay. Feel free to change these percentages up a bit. There's no hard-and-fast rule that you *have* to follow when it comes to writing a budget. Just be sure that you're keeping your catalyst and money goals in mind when you're creating a budget for your family.

Tracking Your Spending

One of my best friends, Amanda, approached me years ago for guidance with her money. She wanted to start budgeting and turned to me for help. I was thrilled to help her set up her budget (I nerd out on this, and the fact that my best friend wanted my support brought me so much joy!). I knew budgeting would help her reach her money goals, but I also knew she needed to start tracking her spending if she wanted to make progress with her money. Amanda needed to know *where* her money was going.

Amanda was on board and willing to do what it took to have confidence with her money. She started tracking her spending and even went back to track where and how she had spent money the month before. I'll never forget the day she called me in complete shock. She had just tracked how much money she and her husband had spent at the grocery store the prior month—and it was *a lot more* than she had expected.

Amanda had never tracked her spending before and assumed they were only spending $400–$500 each month on groceries for the two of them. They both *love* cooking, so going to the grocery store is their version of walking into a theme park with the best rides. As it turns out, she and her husband had spent over $1,000 at the grocery store in one month for just the two of them. They were running by the grocery store every few days, and those quick trips had added up fast.

Needless to say, Amanda's and her husband's eyes were opened after they tracked their spending. She now knew what their biggest temptation was. Even better, she knew that if they wanted to cut back their grocery spending, she would have to put a plan in place to help make that happen.

Amanda and her husband now spend *much less* at the grocery store each month. They have more control over their money, and it all started with both their budget and tracking their spending.

Budgeting and tracking your money go hand in hand. Many people assume they are the same thing, but they are two separate actions.

So, what's the difference between budgeting and tracking?

I'm glad you asked.

When you write a budget, you're making decisions on how to spend your money in the future. You're choosing how much money you *will* spend on dining out, groceries, gas, and all other expenses.

Tracking your spending allows you to categorize and find patterns in your past spending choices. This gives you an idea of how much money you're actually spending on groceries, restaurants, online shopping, clothing, and any other expense in your budget.

I personally love tracking my spending because it provides me with a clear picture of my own personal spending habits. I'm always on the lookout for patterns in my spending. Tracking your spending allows you to identify *where* you tend to overspend as well as *when* you tend to overspend. It also gives you information on whether you're *actually* following the budget you wrote—because let's be honest, we don't always stick to the plan we set.

Many people will download a money app, connect their bank account, and assume they are budgeting. This is a very common mistake. To have complete control over your money, it's important to do both:

- Write a budget for how you *want* to spend your money; and

- Track your past spending to know *where* your money went.

How Should You Track Your Spending?

The easy answer: You get to decide.

The complicated answer: You get to decide. There are *many* options when it comes to tracking your spending and money. The sheer number of apps, spreadsheets, programs, or worksheets can leave you frozen and unable to decide.

When it comes to choosing how you want to track your spending, there are two main considerations to take into place:

1. **Find a system that you can stick to consistently.**

   I once downloaded an app to track my spending. I figured it was an easier way for me to know my money better. The only problem was that I didn't ever *use* the app. It took up space on my phone, and I never logged into it. When the app started sending me the dreaded "You haven't logged in lately; we miss you" emails, I knew it was time to break up with them. The best system is one you can stick to consistently.

2. **Find a system that allows you to categorize your past spending *easily*.**

   The entire purpose of tracking your spending is to look back at your money and see where it went. The goal is to find patterns so that you can set spending boundaries in the future. It's important to be able to categorize your spending in one easy click. Without this feature, you're missing out on one of the main components of tracking your spending.

I personally use a software program on my computer to track our family's spending. While it doesn't come with a savvy app, it's a program that I've been using for the past 15 years (how's that for consistency?) and one that lets me categorize my spending easily.

Because we all have unique personalities and learning styles, what works for me might not work for you, and that's okay. The goal is to find a system that you like. Whether it's an app, spreadsheet, or paper and pencil, just find a system and implement it.

Not sure what type of system you should use to track your spending? Table 3.1 provides a few suggestions broken down by your personality and family dynamic. This will give you a good idea of what to try first. I recommend trying a system for a few months.

If it doesn't work for you, try another system until you find one that sticks.

Tips for finding the best system for you:

- **Apps**: There are *many* apps that you can use to track your spending. Some are free, but the free apps usually have ads. Others have a monthly or yearly fee. Some of the most popular apps include Mint, YNAB, and Truebill. Type "budget app" or "money tracking" into the app store to look through your options.

- **Spreadsheet or software program**: A simple Google search will provide hundreds of choices when it comes to choosing a spreadsheet or software program to track your spending. Choose one that is easy to use and offers support or videos if you need help. I personally use Quicken and have used it for over 15 years.

- **Physical handwritten tracker**: A quick trip to the office supply store or search on Amazon will offer you many options for physical binders you can use to track your spending and budget. You can also search online for downloadable worksheets to create your own binder.

Table 3.1 Determining Your System

For The Person Who Is. . .	System To Try
Always on the go	• Budget or money app
Tech savvy and enjoys data	• Spreadsheet or software program • Budget or money app
A visual learner	• Budget or money app • Physical handwritten tracker
A writer	• Physical handwritten tracker
Managing money with a partner	• Budget or money app • Spreadsheet or software program
Detail oriented	• Spreadsheet or software program • Physical handwritten tracker

You've Tracked Your Spending—Now What?

You've done the work to track your spending. You have the app or program downloaded, and your pay period is over. *Now what?*

This is when most people move on, forget about their spending, and keep living their lives like normal. But you're not most people, are you? *I'm guessing you're not because you're here reading this book.*

Tracking your spending highlights patterns in your spending that you might be blind to. Here are some questions to ask yourself *after* you've categorized your past spending:

- **Did I go over budget in a certain category?** If so, has this been happening for several months in a row? If the answer is yes, it might be time to either increase your budget for that category or put a boundary in place to help you stay on track.

- **Was I caught off guard by any expenses?** Sometimes we're hit with unexpected expenses. These can throw you off budget and leave you frustrated with your money. If any expenses continue to catch you off guard (like that car oil change you forgot you would need), then it's time to think about creating a sinking fund to help cover these costs.

- **What are my strengths and weaknesses?** Don't spend all your time focusing on the areas of your money where you want to improve. Be sure to celebrate the areas where you are strong or have made progress. If you stayed on budget when it came to grocery shopping, recognize and celebrate it. You can also think through areas where you need to improve. If you always end up spending more money on the weekends than you had planned, think about less expensive activities to fill your days off.

If you're willing to track your spending, you'll be amazed at what you learn about yourself and your money. The more you learn, the closer you get to creating helpful money habits that give you the confidence you want and help you reach your goals.

Action Items

- Create your budget:
  - Use a calendar to write out your pay dates;
  - List your fixed expenses;
  - List your variable expenses;
  - List your debts and savings.
- Choose a system to track your spending;
- Ask yourself three questions after tracking your spending:
  - Did I go over budget on a certain category?
  - Was I caught off guard by any expenses?
  - What are my strengths and weaknesses when it comes to spending money?

Chapter 4

The Secret Behind Successful Budgeting

It might surprise you to hear this, but my husband and I still struggle to stick to our budget most months.

Yep. That's right. Here I am, a budget expert confessing that I'm not perfect when it comes to my budget. In fact, I'm far from perfect.

If you struggle with sticking to your budget and making it work for you, you're not alone. People all over the world struggle with the same exact thing. They start a budget and then throw it out the window as soon as they overspend. I totally get it! I've been there many, many times.

In fact, it took giving up on our budget several months in a row to realize that we were falling into a continuous pattern of starting our budget and giving up before our next payday hit. We used every excuse in the book. From "It's my birthday month! Who needs a budget?!" to "We didn't see that medical bill coming. Might as well scrap this month and start over next month."

Matt and I became experts at finding excuses to throw in the towel and start over when it was convenient for us. However, each time we gave up, we hit pause on our money goals. We also weren't being honest with ourselves. If we wanted to change our financial future, then we needed to find a way to make our budget work for us. So, over the years, that's just what we did. It all started with owning the mistakes we were making and coming up with a plan to get back on track with our money.

Three Massive Budget Mistakes to Avoid

If you want to write a successful budget that you can stick to, it's important to avoid the three most massive (and common) budget mistakes. After working with hundreds of people over the years, I've seen the same three mistakes repeated over and over. Most people don't realize they are making these mistakes! I'm speaking from experience because I myself have made all of these mistakes in the past.

When you're aware of what these mistakes are, it's easier to recognize them in yourself and stop making them. Instead, you start making real progress with your money.

Mistake #1: Depriving Yourself and Living on a Supertight Budget

When I was first getting started on my budget journey, I read a book about personal finance. The author advised the reader to cut out *every single* unnecessary item from their budget. They said this was *the key* to living on a budget and paying off debt. After reading the book, I thought, "Wow! This sounds like a great plan! Of course, this is what I need to do!"

This process was great in theory, but I found that over time I started to resent my budget. I realized I still wanted to spend money on what I wanted (yes, even if it was "frivolous"). Because I felt so deprived with my money, I eventually found myself binge spending in the aisles of Target, also known as The Motherland. I walked up and down the aisles of that glorious store and placed everything I wanted, but felt forbidden to buy, in my basket.

Mathematically, *it makes sense* to only spend money on what you *need* in life. In fact, there are tons of books out there that will tell you how to "just spend less money" and cut every single extra expense out of your life.

However, while it makes sense mathematically to cut out all extra spending, it doesn't always make sense *emotionally*.

I wanted to pay off debt, but I also wanted to spend *some* money on things that brought me joy (even if I didn't *need* them). Ultimately, I learned that spending money isn't *bad*. It's okay to spend money on what you love while still saving and reaching your other financial goals.

Money is math, but money is also emotional. We must accept that there are emotions behind our spending and take that into account as well.

If you keep depriving yourself and living on a supertight budget, you're going to give up on your budgeting journey. It's just not sustainable in the long run.

When you stop living on an unrealistic and tight budget, something magical happens! Budgets are no longer a burden. They are no longer this "thing" you do to help you reach your goals. They are no longer a consequence for your past money choices.

When you stop living on an unrealistic and tight budget, you will see your budget and money in a completely different way. Your budget becomes your path to reach your money goals, no matter how big or small they are.

Think back to the previous budgets you've made. Now honestly answer this question: *Did you ever make the mistake of completely depriving yourself and living on an unrealistic budget?*

If you have, that's okay. I've done it too.

From this point on, give yourself room to *live your life* in every budget you write. You can strike a balance between working to meet your money goals and enjoying your life as well. When you write a budget that's realistic for you, your budget becomes something you can actually stick to!

Mistake #2: Losing Traction with Your Budget and Giving Up along the Way

When I first started budgeting, I would write a budget that I thought was perfect. Five days later I would realize my budget was just *not working.*

I felt this way for several reasons:

- There always seemed to be unexpected expenses that threw me completely off budget. How could I stick to a budget when I never knew what expense I'd be hit with?

- There were so many things I wanted to do, and there just didn't seem to be enough money for all of them. How would I decide *what* to spend my money on?

- I didn't want to sacrifice everything. I was an adult who worked hard for her money, and I wanted to spend it on what I wanted.

When this happened, my budget started to feel like my enemy. It was holding me back from enjoying my life, which left me feeling angry and frustrated. I was ready to throw my budget in the trash. This frustration caused me to lose traction with my budget, and I'd ultimately give up along the way.

Has this ever happened to you? Have you ever struggled with getting started on your budget and somehow you end up lost, or off track? Six months later you're thinking, "How did this happen?

I thought I said that this was going to be the year I would manage my money better!"

Why does this happen so much? And how on earth do we stop this cycle?

I believe it's easy to fall off track with your budget in the world we live in today. Social media has led us to be constantly bombarded with ads that are targeted specifically for you. You're also seeing everyone else's highlight reel each time you pick up your phone. Other people seem to be living their best life, going on vacation, and enjoying dinners out.

You're being exposed to ads and other people's best moments each day. This distracts us from our money goals and has us feeling FOMO (fear of missing out). Who wants to miss out? Not me!

Suddenly, a pattern begins to form. You get started with budgeting, decide this time will be different, and eventually become distracted—distracted by others and distracted by your own desires to live your life by your own rules. You eventually lose traction and give up on this entire money journey.

If you continue to give up on budgeting, it's costing you time and progress.

There's only so much time in your life to turn your finances around. Every time you lose traction and give up on your budgeting journey, you're losing precious time that could have been spent shaping your financial future.

Likewise, every time you give up on budgeting, you're losing out on the progress that you could have made with your money. Small progress over time leads to amazing results!

You might even start thinking, "I don't have what it takes to write a budget and be good with money, so why even bother?" When you consistently lose traction with your money and give up, it has a lasting impact on the way you see yourself and money.

What happens when you stop falling into the cycle of losing traction?

When you consistently write a budget you can stick to, you gain the confidence and knowledge that you have what it takes to write a budget that will help you reach your money goals.

Budgeting stops becoming the thing you hate. It stops becoming a thing you dread doing. It stops becoming the thing that keeps you from enjoying your life. Instead, budgeting becomes *the thing* that you look forward to creating. Your budget is now the tool that drives you to pay off debt. It becomes the action that allows you to save money and invest. It's all because you learned how to write a budget that you can stick to and avoid the mistake of losing traction and giving up along the way.

How do you do that? How do stop making the massive mistake of losing traction?

Start by taking a moment to think about what distracts you and causes you to lose focus on your budget. Once you know what is distracting you, it's time to commit to your budget. Just like you would make a commitment to your partner, I want you to commit to following your budget each pay period.

When you're willing to write your budget and see the process through, you gain three amazing things:

1. The confidence that you have what it takes to write a budget for a life you love;

2. Practice with writing budgets that will work for you; and

3. Progress with your money. You'll start saving more money, paying off debt, and seeing results!

It's time to stop losing traction and giving up with your budget—even when it's hard. Even when you're faced with an unexpected expense. Even when you're tempted to throw your budget in the trash.

The only way to see progress with your budget and your money is to consistently work on it each and every day.

Mistake #3: Believing You'll Never Be Good with Money

When I met my husband, he already had the sweetest dog named Joey, which he had rescued from the pound. I must be honest—Joey was *not* the cutest dog out there. Yet he was incredibly kind, patient, loving, and well-behaved. In fact, Joey turned this cat lover into a dog lover!

I had never had a dog before, so when Matt and I moved in together I dreamed about how I would take Joey on walks, teach him tricks, and enjoy my new role as a "dog mom."

The only problem? Joey was not a puppy. He was an adult dog.

At first, I assumed Joey wouldn't be able to learn any new tricks. My daydreams of him happily and obediently responding to my commands and performing adorable tricks faded away. Because you know what they say—*you can't teach an old dog new tricks.*

However, I was determined to work with Joey and teach him a few tricks of my own (even if he was just an old dog). After several days of working with my sweet companion, and *tons* of treats, Joey was able to dance, shake, lay down, and play dead when I pointed at him and yelled "bang!"

Apparently, you *can* teach an old dog new tricks after all.

Isn't that a relief? I personally find it very empowering to know that even a dog can learn something new no matter its age. So what does that mean about us? What does it mean about people who have access to books, the Internet, and a plethora of information? To me, it means you *can* learn something new no matter your age.

The last massive budget mistake to avoid is one that is incredibly common because it stems from your childhood and past relationship with money: believing you'll never be good with money, so why bother trying to budget?

You might be thinking, "Allison, I've never had those thoughts!"

I want you to reexamine what you've told yourself. Many people have these negative thoughts and don't even realize they are playing on repeat in their mind.

This massive mistake, believing you'll never be good with money, can show up in many ways. Maybe you figure that you're an adult and you work hard for your money. You make a decent living—but you feel like you're not making adult decisions. However, you never learned *how* to make adult decisions, so why bother trying to figure it out now?

Maybe you figure you should have learned these personal finance and money lessons sooner. But since no one taught you (and you haven't figured it out yet), you assume you'll never quite get it, so why bother putting forth the effort now? Why bother trying when you've made it this far in life without the right guidance or knowledge for how to handle your money or write a budget? Because you know what they say—*you can't teach an old dog new tricks.*

If you continue to make this massive mistake, it comes at a cost. When you believe you'll never be good with money, it costs you both your confidence and progress on your financial journey.

If you continue to believe you'll never be good with money, you'll continue to feel bad about yourself, your money, and your future.

This massive mistake comes back to our thoughts and how our thoughts can lie to us. The thought "I'm bad with money" is just that: *a thought.* The thoughts that enter your mind are not always true.

If you get stuck believing this lie, you'll have less confidence when it comes to your money. Without confidence, you'll freeze when a money decision or money problem arises. You won't know what to do, how to handle the situation, and ultimately you *pause.* This limiting belief is not only costing you your confidence, but it's also costing you *progress.* How can you move forward with your money if you don't have the confidence that you can achieve something great?

The good news is that you can change the thoughts that enter your mind. You have complete control over what you choose to believe is true. When you stop believing that you'll never be good with money, you start to see that you have what it takes to learn how to handle your finances better. No matter your age. No matter your past. It's at this moment when you start to see and appreciate the amazing results from abandoning this one money lie.

Obviously, simply changing your thoughts won't make money materialize in front of you and erase your money problems. But when you change your thoughts, you are equipping yourself with the confidence to take action in your life and with your money.

Years ago, I believed I would never be good with money. I figured I'd always have debt. But after challenging these lies and choosing to no longer let them hold space in my mind, I found the energy to believe something else. That was when I became determined to learn about budgeting and take steps in a direction that would benefit our family.

Within one year, my husband and I paid off $20,000 worth of debt. We had no inheritances. No high income. No gift money. Just our budget and a strong financial foundation. A foundation that did *not* include the lie that "I'll never be good with money."

The Secret Behind Successful Budgeting

Stop making this massive mistake, and instead choose to believe in yourself. It turns out you can teach an old dog new tricks after all.

How to Stick to Your Budget

One of the most *common* complaints about budgeting comes down to people struggling to *stick* to their budget each month. I know firsthand that self-discipline is easy in theory but can be extremely difficult in real life.

It's no secret that writing a budget isn't the *hardest* part about budgeting. Sticking to your budget and following through with it is where most people struggle. In fact, most budgets fail because people don't see their budget through.

To help make your budget easier to stick to, I'm sharing five tips that you can implement starting today.

Tip #1: Keep a Buffer in Your Budget

Most budgets fail because we expect perfection. However, perfection is *impossible*. Instead of giving up on the process, it's time to expect that unexpected expenses will pop up each month.

Adding a buffer to your budget is a great way to stay on track with your money.

> **A buffer is a line item in your budget that helps cover any miscellaneous spending or unexpected expenses that pop up during your paycheck period.**

The best part? It helps keep you on budget.

When you write your budget each month, add a buffer as a line item. This buffer will help cover any small, unexpected expenses that pop up and tend to get you off track. You can add a buffer to your budget by simply adding the word "buffer" as an item in your budget. Assign an amount for your buffer (our family prefers to add a $100–$200 buffer to every budget). Adding a buffer to your budget will help you stay on budget even when you overspend a little in a few categories.

Tip #2: Stay out of the Stores

When I first started budgeting, I had to have what I like to call a "Target Detox." Essentially, I stayed completely out of Target. Why? Because I had zero self-control inside The Motherland. I knew that if I went into Target, I'd be tempted, so why put myself in that situation?

This might seem a little extreme, but I always told myself that Target would still be there when I was ready and willing to return. It wasn't going anywhere. This fact helped me stick to my detox so I could spend time developing healthier spending habits.

If you're trying to stick to your budget, go to the store as little as possible. This extends to places such as the grocery store and even online shopping. Most people overspend at the grocery store and justify it easily. Instead, only go to the grocery store once a week so you don't have multiple opportunities to spend money that you hadn't planned on spending. You could even consider ordering your groceries online so you don't impulse shop while you're there.

If you struggle with online shopping, it's time to set clear boundaries for when and what you'll buy online, especially since it's almost impossible to "stay out of" an online store. Think about when you're tempted to shop online. Is it late at night when you're feeling bored? If so, find another way to occupy that time. Have "store hours" for yourself when it comes to online shopping. Maybe you'll only shop online once a week for 30 minutes. By setting clear boundaries, you'll be able to stay on track with your budget better.

Overall, you'll spend less money and stick to your budget if you are physically not in a place to spend money. Your wallet and budget will thank you.

Tip #3: Check Your Calendar Before You Make a Budget

Have you ever been completely caught off guard by commitments such as birthday parties, anniversaries, or school functions? You thought you had included every expense in your budget, but somehow you forgot something.

Yeah, me too.

Before you sit down to write your budget, always check your calendar. Check for any celebrations, birthdays, school parties, or social outings that you might attend. Plan for these expenses in advance and budget for them so you don't blow your budget.

I cannot tell you how many times I've had something "unexpected" come up and felt like my budget was off track for the entire month. Once I was off track with my budget, I figured it was a waste of time to keep budgeting. If I'm being completely honest, most of those events were not unexpected at all. I just didn't set aside the time to check my calendar before I wrote my budget. Your budget doesn't have to be completely thrown off track just because your kids had a birthday party to attend or you forgot about end-of-the-year gifts for your child's teacher.

Check your calendar in advance for any and all expenses that might pop up. This will help you stick to your budget during the month.

Tip #4: Track Your Spending Every Day

Many people don't realize just how much money they are spending on food. A lot of times people think they are spending only a certain amount on takeout, but when they add it all up, they are shocked to see how much money they've spent on dinners out.

If you want to stick to your budget, you'll make a point to track where your money is going. Tracking your spending every day forces you to face your financial truth and take an in-depth look at your habits.

Where are you spending the most money?

What are you purchasing that you didn't budget for?

Can you add anything to your budget next month to help ensure that you stay on track?

We've already covered *how* to track your spending, so hopefully you already have a system in place. Now it comes down to choosing a time each day that you'll spend the five minutes completing this eye-opening task.

Tip #5: Find an Accountability Partner

It is crucial to have an accountability partner when you are trying to stick to a budget for the first (or fifth!) time. Your accountability partner can be a spouse, family member, or even a friend.

When you feel like giving up, or you need guidance, turn to your accountability partner for help and encouragement. Celebrate both your big and small wins with this person. Be honest and authentic when it comes to your struggles so they can encourage you. Having someone to walk with on this journey can make getting your money under control much easier.

Of course, there will come a time when you fall off track with your budget. Instead of giving up on your budget completely, it's time to pull out my secret weapon. It's the thing that has made the biggest impact on our money journey and a tool that I wish more people talked about: a mini-budget.

The Secret Weapon to Budgeting: Your Mini-budget

Have you ever written a budget just to throw it away a few days later because something unexpected came up? You created a budget with the best intentions, but then *life happens*. You get carried away swiping your card, and before you know it your budget is blown—again! Or maybe you unintentionally spent too much at the grocery store leaving you with not as much money in your checking account.

Next thing you know, you've thrown your budget in the trash because unexpected expenses or overspending has caused you to lose faith in the plan you had set. You may have even uttered the words, "I'll just start over next month."

Matt and I adopted this habit when we first started budgeting. As soon as something went wrong (because something *always* comes up), we would throw in the towel and vow to do better the next month. The problem was we would immediately overspend and revert to our old money habits. Everything felt like fair game because we no longer had a budget that we were trying to stick to. I would then go on a shopping spree, spend too much money, and justify it by saying we would get back on track next pay period. Ultimately, these habits were keeping us from reaching our financial goals sooner.

It only took a few months of repeatedly starting over to realize we were setting ourselves up for failure. At that moment, I realized that our budget would never be perfect. And guess what? That's totally okay.

Budgeting is less about the math and more about your flexibility and willingness to stick with it. Instead of starting over the next month, we started writing mini-budgets to help us get back on track with our money. Mini-budgets have saved our family's finances month after month. They have given me peace of mind and have allowed me to have more control over my finances.

A mini-budget is a smaller budget that you write from today until your next payday, no matter how long the timeframe is.

A mini-budget helps you take back control of your budget when you've gotten off track. Instead of throwing the budget out the window, create a mini-budget to help you get back on track with your financial goals.

How to Write a Mini-budget

The best part about a mini-budget is that it's incredibly easy to write. I've been known to write a mini-budget on a sticky note and keep it on the fridge for five days until payday hits.

Here are the simple steps to follow to write your first mini budget:

1. **Write down the current balance in your checking account.**

   After overspending and getting off budget, you might be tempted to avoid or ignore this first step. It might scare you to look at your checking account balance because you know you'll feel a tinge of guilt and frustration with your choices. *If you ignore the problem, it doesn't exist, right?*

   Wrong. That's what we like to think to ease the stress of dealing with the problem, but it couldn't be farther from the truth.

   Sit down, pull out your phone, and open your online banking app. Write down your balance. If you have any pending transactions, be sure to deduct those from the balance. This number is your starting point.

2. **Determine how many days you have until your next payday.**

Look at your calendar and determine when your next payday is. How many days do you have from today until that date? Write that number down. The number of days until your next payday is how long your mini-budget will last. I've written a mini-budget that lasts fourteen days as well as a mini-budget that lasts me three days until payday.

3. List out your expenses.

Make a list of expenses you expect to have from now until payday. Don't forget to include bills that are automatically drafted from your bank account. If you aren't sure which bills you have coming up, look at your last month's bank statement for guidance.

Be sure to check your calendar and make sure you don't have any events coming up that you'll need to budget for such as birthdays, parties, or special events with friends. Include any variable expenses such as groceries, gas, and restaurants in your mini-budget.

I personally like to think through each day until my next payday. I ask myself whether I anticipate spending money on that particular day. If the answer is yes, I include it in my mini-budget.

Your goal is to create a plan for your money until payday, even if payday is only a few days away.

4. Create your mini-budget.

Create a mini-budget using the money you have left in your account and the expenses you listed. You can jot your mini-budget down on a spare piece of paper, sticky note, or even a budget page. I personally find handwriting my mini-budget helps solidify my expectations for my money in my brain.

5. Post your budget where you can see it every day.

Once you've written your mini-budget, you *need* to post it where you can see it. Don't keep it tucked away in a binder or on an Excel spreadsheet. It's important that this budget is visible and at the top of your mind.

Go back and reference your mini-budget often. If you find yourself off track again, write another mini-budget.

Here's an example of a mini-budget:

Checking account balance: $400.00

Mini-budget dates: March 9–14

Expenses:

- Groceries: $100

- Gas: $40

- Electricity bill: $200

- Restaurants: $50

- Buffer: $10

Total: $400.00

It's that simple! The mini-budget above lays out how much money is left in this person's checking account as well as where every penny will be going.

Three Benefits of a Mini-budget

Yes, a mini-budget may take you time to write, even if it's just a few minutes. But the benefits of sitting down to write your mini-budget far outweigh the small time commitment.

Here are the three main benefits that I've seen mini-budgets have not just in my life but others' as well.

1. Mini-budgets allow you to continue making progress— even after life happens.

Mini-budgets help you continue to make forward progress with your money—even when you've been hit with unexpected expenses and you'd rather give up on budgeting altogether. Instead of giving up, you're getting back on track. You recognize the problem and you set out to fix it instead of just saying you'll start over next month.

Giving up is easy. Writing a mini-budget and getting back on track is where the real work and growth lies.

2. Mini-budgets hold you accountable.

Mini-budgets are amazing because not only do they hold you accountable for your finances, but they also give you the opportunity to learn how to be flexible with your money. No one is perfect, and no budget is perfect. Every budget will need to be tweaked every now and then.

I personally love that mini-budgets allow us to identify what went wrong with our previous budget and how to take steps to prevent that from happening in the future. Writing a mini-budget is not about beating yourself up or giving yourself a hard time for your past spending. Instead, it's an opportunity to manage your money better.

3. Mini-budgets set you up for success.

I personally try to cook dinner at home five or six nights each week. The only problem? I don't really like cooking. In fact, I would go so far as to say I "strongly dislike" cooking dinner. While others find comfort in the kitchen, creating a lovely meal for their family, I simply cannot stand it.

Yet every week I cook dinner for my family (my husband helps too). The *only* way I'm able to stay somewhat consistent with cooking dinner at home is because I spend time on the weekend planning out the dinners I will make that week. I *always* plan easy meals on Thursday because those are the days I'm tempted to order pizza just to stay out of the kitchen.

My meal plan sets me up for success. It's *the thing* that keeps me on track with cooking healthy, simple meals for my family instead of grabbing takeout every night. Just like I need a meal plan to help me be successful when it comes to cooking at home, we need a mini-budget to help us be successful with our money.

When you are willing to write a mini-budget after you fall off track with your money, you'll be more aware of where you stand financially and how you can continue to grow closer to your money goals.

We all know ignoring your finances won't make them any better. When you are willing to spend time working on your money, you begin to develop better financial habits that can have a lasting impact on your life.

Action Items

- Ask yourself if your budget is *realistic*;
- Add pocket money to your budget;
- Add a buffer to your budget;
- Find an accountability partner to share your budget and money goals with; and
- Write a mini-budget when you get off track.

Chapter 5

Paying Off Debt While Enjoying Life

My close friend Kendra came to me one day after work and told me that she needed help. She had the courage to put her own pride and fear of judgment aside to openly share her financial struggles with me. She was vulnerable enough to lay it all out. The good, the bad, and the ugly.

Kendra and her husband, Marco, had just found out they were expecting another baby. While they were thrilled with this news, they were shocked to realize that they wouldn't have enough money each month to cover daycare costs when their daughter arrived.

I soon learned that daycare costs were the least of their worries. Kendra and Marco were drowning in debt. They had student loans, car debt, medical debt, and credit card debt. They were barely making ends meet every single month. As a result, Kendra was suffering from high financial anxiety that would lead to full-blown anxiety attacks at times.

Kendra's fear of what their account balance would say was stronger than her desire to know the truth. Instead of looking at their checking account, she would ask Marco for a rundown of their finances. He assured her they would be fine. While she wanted to believe him, she knew deep down that something *had* to change.

Marco is one of the most positive and optimistic people I've ever met. He believes everything will eventually work out in the end. Any time Kendra expressed concern over their finances, Marco was right there to assure her it would all be okay.

While Marco was an incredibly positive person, he was also a serious spender. He lived the life he dreamed of, but the way he did so led to significant credit card debt. If a credit card company increased his credit limit, he saw that as money in their pocket. This view on credit cards led them deeper into credit card debt over time.

Kendra didn't know *how* to talk about her financial fears with Marco and get him to see their money the same way she did. She thought he would listen to someone else, someone who had been in his shoes before.

Kendra asked if I would sit down with them and work through their finances together. She wanted a plan. A plan that would allow them to have money for daycare once their daughter arrived. I said I would do it under one condition: that Marco comes to the table with an open mind.

A Turning Point

Two weeks later I was sitting at their dining room table. The three of us huddled around my laptop screen. I had created a spreadsheet where we listed out Kendra and Marco's finances in detail.

We started with their debt payments and listed out the balance, minimum payment, and interest rates for each debt they had. Next, we listed out every monthly expense they were paying at the time. We talked about which expenses were necessary, unnecessary, and which expenses they could shop around for a better price. Finally, we discussed their spending habits. We had an open and honest conversation about *why* Marco liked to spend money and how this spending affected Kendra's anxiety as well as their bank account.

Together, this couple developed a plan where Marco could still spend money but within a boundary they both felt comfortable with.

We created a step-by-step plan that felt doable for both of them. They finally knew exactly *how* they would be able to pay off over $103,000 of debt. I'm happy to say that Kendra and Marco are now working on paying off their final credit card as I'm writing this book.

Kendra's financial anxiety that plagued her for years completely disappeared. Marco no longer saw his credit card as an open invitation to buy whatever he wants.

And the icing on the cake? They both felt empowered and in control of their money for the first time in their lives. They have learned how to communicate effectively about one of the biggest aspects of their life: money.

This couple is finally on the same page. Both Kendra and Marco are excited for what's next on their financial journey. It all started with the courage to set pride aside and seek guidance.

You might relate to part of Marco and Kendra's story. You might wish that you too could turn to someone for help and guidance when it comes to paying off debt. Don't worry, I've got you covered.

Paying off debt opens doors and gives you *options* when it comes to your life that you wouldn't have otherwise. It frees up your money so you can keep your entire paycheck and spend it how you want. Being debt free allows you to give generously, spend based on your values, and erases the financial stress that might be suffocating you.

When it comes to paying off debt, it's best to choose a plan and stick with it. Consistency is key! Let's pick the plan that will work best for you and your unique family.

Debt Payoff Strategies

You've decided you want to become debt free. *Now what?*

A simple Google search will bring up hundreds if not thousands of articles filled with ideas, strategies, and ways to become debt free. All that information can be so overwhelming that you might not even know where to begin.

That's why I'm breaking down two very common ways to pay off debt as well as the debt payoff method that Marco and Kendra used. This way you'll be able to confidently decide which method will work for you and your journey.

The Debt Snowball Method

Imagine a ball of snow rolling down a hill. As it continues to roll, it picks up more snow and grows larger by the second. Eventually, the small ball of snow you started with has become a massive force to be reckoned with. This is the illustration behind the debt snowball method.

The debt snowball method is a system of paying off debt in order from the smallest loan balance to the largest loan balance. When you pay off a debt, you'll take the minimum payment from it and add that amount to your payment for the next debt. With the elimination of each consecutive loan, the amount of money you're able to send to the next one grows just like a snowball grows as you roll it down the hill. Eventually you are left with one large payment for your final and largest debt.

How the Debt Snowball Works

I love a good step-by-step plan. Here's exactly how the debt snowball works:

1. List out all your debts from the *smallest balance to the largest balance.* Don't worry about minimum payments or interest rates.

2. Make the minimum payment on each loan. Pay any extra money you can to your smallest debt.

3. Find extra money by budgeting, working an extra job, or selling things around your house that you don't need. Immediately send that money to your smallest debt.

4. Once you pay off your smallest debt, take that monthly payment and add it to your next smallest debt payment.

5. Pay off your next debt (way to go!).

6. Keep the process rolling until you have one last debt. Pay it off and celebrate!

Table 5.1 gives an example of the debt snowball method in action. In the example in Table 5.1, you would start by paying off the AMEX credit card. Once that debt has been paid off, you would roll the $35 minimum payment into the next debt on your list, the personal loan. Your new payment for the personal loan would be $124 + $35, which is $159.00. Continue to follow this pattern until you're left with one final debt payment.

Table 5.1 Debt Snowball Example

Payoff Order	Loan Name	Loan Balance	Minimum Payment	Snowball Payment
1	AMEX Credit Card	$550.00	$35.00	
2	Personal Loan	$982.00	$124.00	$35.00 + $124.00 = $159.00
3	Car Loan #1	$3,421.00	$296.50	$159.00 + $296.50 = $455.50
4	Visa Credit Card	$4,857.00	$107.00	$455.50 + $107.00 = $562.50
5	Car Loan #2	$18,309.00	$427.00	$562.50 + $427.00 = $989.50
6	Student Loan	$32,006.00	$339.50	$989.50 + $339.50 = $1,329.00
	Total	**$60,125.00**	**$1,3929.00**	

Paying Off Debt While Enjoying Life

By the time you reach your final debt, you're left with the ability to make one large payment each month. Take it from someone who paid off debt using the debt snowball method, getting to that point was *incredible!*

Our family personally chose to use the debt snowball method because we desperately needed to free up cash flow each month before our baby arrived. The interest rates on our debts were all under 7%, which meant we didn't have any high-interest debt hanging over us.

We knew that experiencing quick progress and celebrating a few small wins right away would give us the momentum to keep going, especially since this journey would take us over four years. With that in mind, we decided to follow the debt snowball method. I cannot tell you how incredible it felt to pay off our very first debt. It may have been a small student loan, but it was gone forever. The exhilaration that came from our progress motivated us to tackle the next debt on our list.

By the time we were paying off our last debt, we were able to send almost $2,000 each month to our final loan. It is amazing to see just how much progress you can make when you follow the debt snowball method!

The Debt Snowball: Pros and Cons

Of course, there are pros and cons to each debt payoff method. It's important to weigh these pros and cons and then choose the method that is best for you and your family. Not everyone will pay off debt the same way, and that's 100% okay.

Debt Snowball Pros:

- The debt snowball method provides you with an easy win by paying off your smallest loan first. These smaller wins at the beginning give you the motivation to keep going and see progress on your journey.

- The debt snowball method is easy to implement. Simply go down the list when it comes to paying off debt. No headaches or complexity here.

Debt Snowball Cons:

- Because you don't take interest rates into consideration when you use the debt snowball method, you might be paying more interest on some of your larger loans along the way. For instance, if your smallest loan only has a 4% interest rate but your larger loan has a 24% interest rate, you'll make slower progress on your larger loans.

- Mathematically, following the debt snowball method *could* take longer on your debt-free journey, especially if you have high-interest debt that you don't pay off right away.

The debt snowball method is an ideal plan for anyone that is just getting started on their debt-free journey and is desperate to see results right away. When you can pay off debt quickly and experience success right out of the gate, you're motivated to keep working on your finances.

Remember, money is math, but money is also emotional. The debt snowball method appeals to the emotions of money.

The Debt Avalanche Method

While the debt snowball method ignores interest rates for loans, the debt avalanche method does the exact opposite: it focuses solely on the interest rates of your loans. **The debt avalanche method is a system for paying off debt in order from the highest interest rate loan to the lowest interest rate loan.**

Mathematically, this allows you to pay less in interest over time because you're tackling the highest interest debt first.

Paying Off Debt While Enjoying Life

How the Debt Avalanche Works

Here's exactly how the debt avalanche method works, step-by-step:

1. List all your debts from the highest interest rate to the lowest interest rate.

2. Make the minimum payment on each loan. Send any extra money you can to your loan with the highest interest rate.

3. Find extra money by budgeting, working an extra job, or selling things around your house that you don't need. Immediately send that money to your debt with the highest interest rate.

4. As you pay off your debts, take that monthly payment and add it to your next highest interest rate loan.

5. Pay off your next debt (way to go!).

6. Keep going until you have only one loan left, the one with the lowest interest!

Table 5.2 gives an example of the debt avalanche method.

Table 5.2 Debt Avalanche Example

Payoff Order	Loan Name	Loan Balance	Minimum Payment	Interest Rate
1	AMEX Credit Card	$550.00	$35.00	27.6%
2	Visa Credit Card	$4,857.00	$107.00	24.9%
3	Personal Loan	$982.00	$124.00	9.7%
4	Car Loan #1	$3,421.00	$296.50	8.5%
5	Student Loan	$32,006.00	$339.50	6.2%
6	Car Loan #2	$18,309.00	$427.00	2.9%
	Total	**$60,125.00**	**$1,3929.00**	

Just like the debt snowball method, you'll want to take the previous minimum payment and use it on your next debt to pay off each debt faster. This method will save you the most money overall because you'll be paying off the debt with the highest interest rate first.

The Debt Avalanche: Pros and Cons

Just like the debt snowball method, the debt avalanche method also has its own set of pros and cons.

Debt Avalanche Pros:

- Because you're focusing on paying off high-interest debt first, you'll end up sending less money to debt in the long run. The faster you pay off those high-interest loans, the better off you are.
- Mathematically, this is the quickest way to pay off debt. It could even shorten your debt-free journey by several months in some cases.

Debt Avalanche Cons:

- The debt avalanche method requires discipline and focus right off the bat. You might not experience a win right away (especially if your highest interest rate debt has a large balance). The longer it takes you to have that success, the easier it is to give up on your debt payoff journey.
- The debt avalanche method requires extra money each month. If you want to send a lot of money toward your highest interest debt *while* making minimum payments on your other debts, you'll need extra money that you can earmark for that loan. Some people just don't have that extra money lying around at the beginning of their journey.

The debt avalanche method is an ideal plan for anyone who is driven, disciplined, and finds motivation from knowing that this is the fastest method to pay off debt. If you want to pay off debt *fast* and you're willing to wait longer to experience your first win, then you'll love the debt avalanche method!

The DIY Debt Payoff Method

Your debt payoff journey doesn't have to be a cookie-cutter experience that follows a certain set of rules. You *can* create your own plan to follow, one that will work well for your family.

That's exactly what Kendra and Marco had to do. They needed a plan that fit their specific needs. Their main priority was to free up enough cash flow each month to pay for upcoming daycare expenses. To do this, we created their own unique debt payoff plan, which I like to call the DIY debt payoff method.

Kendra and Marco's plan focused on eliminating their debts with the highest monthly payments, but lowest balances first. This way, by the time their precious daughter arrived, they had enough money left over each month to put her in daycare once Kendra returned to work.

The DIY debt payoff method is a debt payoff plan that you create yourself based on your own unique needs and wants. It is a plan that you put together yourself because it makes sense for your family. It allows you to take into consideration your unique situation, needs, and goals. There are no rules you need to follow when you do it yourself (DIY) for your debt payoff plan. The only thing that matters is how you *want* to pay off debt.

How The DIY Debt Payoff Method Works

The idea of creating your own DIY debt payoff plan doesn't have to be complicated. Here are the steps we followed to help Kendra and Marco create their own DIY Debt Payoff plan.

1. List all your debts on a piece of paper. Include the balance, minimum monthly payment, and interest rate.

2. Think about your family's goals. Ask yourself these questions:

   a. What do you want to accomplish?

   b. Are you trying to free up cash flow or money for an upcoming expense?

   c. What debt do you wish you could see gone first?

3. Choose the order in which you will pay off each debt. Number each debt starting with a 1 all the way until you've assigned every debt a number. This is the order you'll pay off debt.

4. Make the minimum payment on each loan. Send any extra money you can to the first loan on your DIY debt payoff plan.

5. Find extra money by budgeting, working an extra job, or selling things around your house that you don't need. Immediately send that money to the debt you're working to pay off.

6. As you pay off your debts, take that monthly payment and add it to the next debt on your list.

7. Pay off your next debt (way to go!).

8. Keep going until you have only one loan left!

If you're a visual learner like me, it can be helpful to see the DIY debt payoff method in action. Table 5.3 is an example of the DIY debt payoff method.

In Table 5.3, the personal loan has been moved up to the first spot in the debt payoff plan. This could be for several reasons. Maybe the personal loan has a cosigner on it and the person who has the debt wants to pay it off so the cosigner no longer has this extra headache. Another possible explanation could be that the minimum payment is higher, but the balance isn't very high. It wouldn't be too

Table 5.3 DIY Debt Payoff Example

Payoff Order	Loan Name	Loan Balance	Minimum Payment	Interest Rate
1	Personal Loan	$982.00	$124.00	9.7%
2	AMEX Credit Card	$550.00	$35.00	27.6%
3	Visa Credit Card	$4,857.00	$107.00	24.9%
4	Car Loan #1	$3,421.00	$296.50	8.5%
5	Car Loan #2	$18,309.00	$427.00	2.9%
6	Student Loan	$32,006.00	$339.50	6.2%
	Total	**$60,125.00**	**$1,3929.00**	

hard to pay off this $982 loan and it would free up an extra $124 each month.

Once you're adding the $124 minimum to the $35 minimum for the credit card payment, you'll quickly have paid off the highest interest item on the list. Then, you add that $159 to the $107 for the other credit card and eliminate your next highest interest rate item on the list.

After that, an interesting thing happens. Both car loans are paid off before the student loan, even though the student loan has a higher rate than one of the car loans. Maybe you've decided that car loans are recurring loans that happen every so often, so you want to get them paid off before it's time for the next one. Maybe you've seen the size of that student loan and recognized that it will take a while to pay it off, and you want to make faster progress with your other loans.

This method gives you the freedom to decide *how* you will pay off debt. It allows you to take into consideration more than just the minimum balance and interest rate of each loan.

The DIY Debt Payoff: Pros and Cons

The DIY debt payoff method has its own pros and cons just like the debt snowball and debt avalanche method. These should be taken into consideration before you implement this method.

DIY Debt Payoff Pros:

- The DIY debt payoff method gives you full control over how you pay off debt. This allows you to create a plan that matches your current situation.

- If you are paying off debt with a partner, the DIY debt payoff plan offers an opportunity to compromise on how you will pay off debt together. Each person can choose a debt that is important to them to pay off and ultimately each person feels seen and heard.

DIY Debt Payoff Cons:

- The DIY debt payoff plan takes a little more work to get going. You must truly understand your financial situation and make important decisions when it comes to paying off debt. There's more thinking and planning that goes into this method.

- Some people want a plan handed to them. They want to follow a step-by-step system that has been proven to work. The DIY debt payoff plan requires you to create your own system. This can be overwhelming to some people.

The DIY debt payoff method is ideal for you if you want full ownership and say in *how* you pay off debt. It's ideal for the family that wants to pay off debt on their own terms and in a specific order that might not be traditional. It's great for those who want to pay off a debt that has been bothering them emotionally for years on end, like a credit card or family loan.

No matter how you decide to pay off debt, it's important to remember that every person's debt-free journey will be different. What worked for me, Marco and Kendra, or one of your friends might not work for you. And guess what? That's totally okay! We are all unique.

Whichever method you choose, the good news is that you're one step closer to making progress on your debt-free journey!

Your Debt Payoff Plan

No matter *how* you decide to pay off debt, it's important to sit down and physically write out your plan. Why? Because writing out your plan on paper solidifies it in your mind. Plus, if you're on this journey with a partner, it ensures you are both on the same page.

Fill out the My Debt Payoff Plan Worksheet to organize how you will pay off debt. You can also download a free PDF version of this worksheet at www.inspiredbudget.com/moneymadeeasy:

My Debt Payoff Plan

Payoff Order	Loan Name	Loan Balance	Minimum Payment	Interest Rate
	Total			

Paying Off Debt While Enjoying Life

Once you've filled out the My Debt Payoff Plan Worksheet, print it out and post it somewhere so you see it often. This way, paying off debt and your plan are at the forefront of your mind.

I personally kept the My Debt Payoff Plan Worksheet posted on my closet door. This was an area in our home that I visited every day but was also private and wouldn't be seen by guests.

How to Pay Off Debt and Save Money at the Same Time

I'm so excited that you want to pay off debt. Making that decision is big and will have a huge impact on your finances from here on out. But what about saving money? *Should you still send money to savings and retirement while tackling debt?*

Our family faced this same question while we were on our debt-free journey, and many others have written to ask me what they should do as well. There are countless opinions on what you should be doing while you're paying off debt. Some people say to stop saving money altogether. Others say it's still smart to continue saving and investing.

Here's the truth: you can save money while paying off debt! We did, and so many others have as well! Let's break down *how* to save money while still paying off debt.

1. Don't Ignore Your Budget

Many people liken the idea of writing a budget to not getting what they want. However, a budget is simply a plan for your money. You can still buy what you want. You can still spend money where your heart desires. It just all comes down to what you can afford.

If you haven't already, it's time to write a budget for your current pay period. Remember that learning how to write a budget that fits your life might take time. Just like it takes time to learn how to ride a bike, it will take time and practice to learn how to write (and stick to) your budget.

When you make budgeting a habit, you will find ways to send extra money to debt and savings. It will show you where you're spending money and help you determine how you can pay off debt faster. Before you do anything, set up your budget. I *promise* that it's key to your money success.

2. Set Up an Emergency Fund

Before you even think about sending extra money toward your debt payments, you'll want to save money for your emergency fund. We will dive deeper into your emergency fund in the next chapter, but I must stress that you should *not* skip over this step.

Setting aside money in an emergency fund (even $1,000 per person in your family) will keep you from accruing more debt while you're on your debt-free journey. Somewhere along the way, *something will go wrong*.

Whether a rock suddenly hits your windshield while driving down the freeway, or you chip a tooth unexpectedly, life will happen whether or not you're financially prepared. Having money in a savings account for emergencies and unexpected expenses will keep you from taking out another loan or putting large expenses on your credit card.

The goal in all this is to get out of debt, not go back into it!

3. Start Saving Money for What You Know You'll Need

While you're sending extra money to pay off debt, it's important to still save money for what you know you'll need in the future. For instance, it's a great idea to set aside money each month for Christmas or holidays. This way, when December rolls around, you aren't going into debt to buy gifts.

To help you save money while paying off debt, add these types of savings as line items in your budget. For instance, our family saves money *every* month for our yearly HOA dues and flood insurance. One of the items on our budget page reads "HOA dues and flood insurance." Instead of being caught off guard when our HOA dues and insurance must be paid in January, we transfer $150 to a savings account each month. This way when January comes around, we have all the money we need to cover these yearly home expenses.

4. Pause Extra Debt Payments When Emergencies Happen

We all know that emergencies will happen. You should expect them. There will be plenty of times when you'll need to use your emergency fund. One of my friends was working on paying off debt when she noticed a few bugs flying near her ceiling. After a quick glance she realized they were what every homeowner fears: termites. Not the news she wanted to hear! Thankfully, the termites hadn't created too much damage, and she was able to use her emergency fund to have her home professionally treated.

She was beyond thankful that she had the money to cover this unexpected home cost. Once her home was termite-free she focused her attention on filling her emergency fund back up.

Instead of sending extra money toward her debt payments, she paid the minimum on all her loans. Any extra penny she could find, she sent to her savings account. As soon as her emergency fund was back to where she liked it, she started working to pay off debt again.

One thing we can expect in life is that unexpected expenses will pop up. Your savings account will be used while you're paying off debt. Just know that this is completely okay. It's there for a reason.

5. Continue to Contribute to Retirement

When it comes to investing, the sooner you start, the better off you'll be. Many people ask themselves the same question: *Should you invest for retirement while paying off debt?*

There are many opinions around this. To be honest, it's going to depend on your unique situation. It's important to take into consideration how many years you have until retirement, how much debt you have, as well as if you have any high-interest debt.

No matter what, it's important to know your options. Below are four options to consider.

- **Option A**: Pay off all your debt first and then invest. This is a great option for someone who has a smaller amount of debt and can pay it off within a few months.

- **Option B**: Invest up to your 401(k) match (if you receive one) and then pay off debt. Your match is free money. Meeting the match allows you to invest as well as have your company contribute to your retirement.

- **Option C**: Pay off all your high-interest debt first and then invest while you pay off your lower interest debt. If you have any credit cards or high-interest debt (10%+), then you could pay that off fast and then start investing.

- **Option D**: Do both. It's easy to ignore retirement, especially if it's far away. But when it comes to investing for retirement, *time is your best friend*. The longer your money has to grow, the bigger impact it will have on your future.

There's no doubt about it—you *can* save money and pay off debt at the same time. In fact, I recommend that you do just that! Saving money while paying off debt will prepare you for any unexpected expenses that might come your way. It will also keep you from going further into debt when life throws you a curve ball.

How to Stay Motivated While Paying Off Debt

Here's the truth. Wherever any of us are on our debt-free journey, we all face discouragement, reluctance, or flat-out caving when it comes to following through with our commitments and meeting our goals. That's why debt payoff motivation is so important.

As crazy as it may sound, it's not a question of *if* we'll need motivation but *when* we'll need motivation. Even the best intentions and a can-do spirit can often give way to despair if we aren't mindful about our own approach to getting rid of debt once and for all.

You may be on fire about getting out of debt and can't imagine needing any more motivation than that. But that enthusiasm can flicker over time in the long run. In order to keep that enthusiasm going, I have some tips and tricks to keep that fire burning for months (or years) to come.

1. Keep Your Progress Visual

Nothing motivates people more than visually seeing the progress they've made, and it's especially true for debt payoff motivation. As debt shrinks, the stress lifts! Progress helps to build momentum and keeps your eyes on the prize.

The best way to track your progress and allow it to drive you farther on your debt-free journey is to make it visual. Any graphic representation will do, but you may have your own specific preferences or twists on how to illustrate your progress.

The important thing about this is that you can see it, and it illustrates positive movement.

It's nice to have a dream board and visualize the end result, but it's more important to celebrate the everyday small steps that you take along the way. If you like to visualize the end and you have a clear image of what being debt free would be like, use that. Make that image literal. Print it out. Cut it up to pieces and make it into a puzzle. It can be a 20-piece puzzle or 100. The important thing is that each piece of the puzzle represents a block of progress that you have made, so when you reach your goal, you also complete the picture and have simultaneously fully realized your dream.

To keep myself motivated on our debt-free journey, I created a thermometer that I would color in as we would pay off debt. Every few months I would question *why* we were paying off debt. My motivation would waver, and I would be ready to give up.

It was in that moment that I would update our debt-free thermometer. As I grabbed my red Sharpie and started coloring in our debt-free thermometer, I could see how much money we had paid off. This simple visual gave me the motivation that I was missing to keep going on our journey.

2. Stay Updated on Your Numbers

Let's face it. Some of us are numbers people, and some of us aren't. But, unfortunately, in order to make your dream of being debt free a reality, you have to be a little bit of a numbers person.

Don't worry! There's good news here. This doesn't require you to be good at math (enter a collective sigh of relief here). It does mean that you may have to train yourself to look at numbers more often, however.

The trade-off is worth it. By doing this, you will unlock a level of debt payoff motivation that avoiding numbers simply cannot help you with.

> **When you boil it all down, debt is an equation, and equations are solved with numbers. The way you succeed on your debt-free journey is by changing those numbers in meaningful ways.**

Change what you make. Change what you pay for this or that. Reduce costs, eliminate costs. It all has the potential to be exciting when you see how your equation starts to result in a $0 balance (or more!) at the end. Staying on top of your numbers might sound tedious at first, but it can become an addiction that will keep you motivated to keep moving toward your goal of a debt-free life.

3. Make Every Step Count

Mapping progress and visually seeing improvement are so essential to motivation that it can't be overstated. **The times you need the most debt payoff motivation are the times when you feel you've slipped and have lost progress.** However, that just shows how important progress is in your overall mood and attitude.

Keep up your momentum by making calculated moves to continue gaining an edge over your debt. When it comes to paying off debt, every step counts. You can do this in a variety of ways. Opting to cook dinner and save $30 to put toward your debt is a big deal and counts toward your debt-free journey. Canceling cable and only subscribing to a few streaming services might seem minuscule, but it makes an impact while you're paying off debt.

Don't discount the small steps that make big moves on your debt-free journey. Celebrate these small steps, and use them to fuel your motivation.

4. Make More Aggressive Moves

If you are the type to tackle higher interest debt first, you may be a fan of making bold, aggressive moves. The slow and steady approach will get you where you want to go incrementally, but sometimes a big, dramatic move is just the action you need to stay motivated.

There is a rush you get when you transfer a large sum of money to knock out a debilitating interest rate. Or when you take on another income source to pay down debt faster. Freezing your spending accounts, canceling subscriptions, and negotiating with creditors can each make a big impact on your bottom line.

Large chunks of debt get demolished, making the end feel closer and more attainable. That, in turn, creates more debt payoff motivation.

5. Stay on Your Feet

Let's not lose sight of the fact that we are human. As important as it is to optimize our budget, we should remember that we all falter at some point. Losing traction, or losing an edge, is not losing the war. It's at times when we find ourselves slipping that we need to stay the course and not lose hope.

Overemphasizing mistakes or being overly critical has a backward effect. It can lead to a loss of motivation if you slip up and spend too much or use your money less effectively than you could have. The irony here is that if you submit to that sense of defeat, you will continue to backslide and take yourself farther from your goal.

At times like this, you can find your debt payoff motivation by looking at how far you have already come on your debt-free journey. One great way to do that is to keep your charts, graphs, spreadsheets, dream boards, lists, and so on as you pay off each debt. Don't throw them out. When you're feeling down, look at all of your accomplishments. The two best motivators are looking ahead at where you want to be and looking back at how you successfully moved from where you don't want to be. You've got this.

6. Create Incentives for Debt Payoff Motivation

A very easy way to continually encourage yourself while you climb out of debt is to include little incentives for reaching benchmark goals on the way to eliminating debt. A small reward here and there is excellent debt payoff motivation as long as it doesn't hurt your overall progress too much.

You can indulge yourself in some way that is either free or the cost is built into your budget plan. When you work your numbers, give yourself room to splurge a little bit when a goal has been met. Not only will this motivate you to reach that next benchmark, but it will also allow you to let off some steam in a way that is planned.

This way, there's not a negative effect on your progress that could send you spiraling into hopeless despair. Instead, it gives you a chance to breathe for a moment, bask in your accomplishment, and then get right back to work on reaching your next target.

7. Grow a Savings Balance While You Pay Down Debt

Sometimes paying off debt can feel like throwing money into a bottomless hole. Especially if that debt doesn't seem to move enough right away.

But you don't want to make that hole worse by continuing to spend money you don't have, thereby generating even more interest on credit cards and loans. One rule I love to use is the pay yourself first model.

If you can find it in your budget to set a little bit of money aside each month in a savings account, it can provide huge debt payoff motivation! Paying yourself does not mean treating yourself, though.

That money should be invested, first in a savings account and later in a retirement account or other higher interest investment.

Growing a balance of saved income while paying off debt is exciting because you can see it accrue over time, and once you are debt free, that savings account balance will still be there bigger than ever, to start everything over with.

Watching your savings account get bigger each month even while you pay down debt helps to give you a sense of confidence and ensures that you have enough money for emergency expenses without having to fall further behind on debt.

8. Stay Motivated with Inspiring Quotes

When all else fails, I like to turn to a good inspiring quote to keep me motivated in life. I write them on sticky notes on my mirror, put them in my notepad on my iPhone, and doodle with them on the side of my budget notebook. It really does help reignite my motivation!

You can find inspiring quotes by using a quick Google search. These can work wonders when it comes to keeping you on track with your debt payoff goal.

Rethink Your Debt-free Journey

If you're paying off debt, it's important to change the way you think about your debt-free journey. Many people enter this journey with a negative mindset and eventually feel deprived or entitled to a different life. While they might get started with paying off debt, their negative outlook causes them to lose traction and give up.

Instead of falling into that crowd, I want you to rethink your debt-free journey. While it may not be fun, find the good that it brings into your life. Paying off debt has countless benefits.

Personally speaking, paying off debt for 4.5 years taught our family many lessons. We learned how to:

- Prioritize what we want in life—not everything holds the same weight and value;

- Have patience when it comes to spending and saving money;

- Have difficult but necessary conversations as a couple working toward the same goal;

- Teach our kids to save, have patience, and live on a budget.

- Identify what we value spending money on. While we can't have *everything* we want in life, this journey taught us what we want *most* when it comes to our money.

This journey won't be easy, but I *promise* you that it will be worth it. You can do this!

Action Items

- Choose the debt payoff plan that will work for your family:
  - Debt snowball method;
  - Debt avalanche method; or
  - DIY debt payoff method.
- Fill out the My Debt Payoff Plan Worksheet.
- Begin saving money while paying off debt at the same time. Add these savings goals as line items in your budget.
- Find ways to stay motivated on your debt-free journey when you want to give up.

Chapter 6

Saving for Emergencies

When our youngest son, James, was three years old, he had what we assumed was a simple stomach virus. My husband and I kept him home from daycare, cuddled with him all day, and did our best to help him get better. It wasn't until the next day at 11:00 p.m. that my gut told me something else was wrong. This wasn't *just* a stomach virus—it was something bigger.

I was lying next to him in bed while he slept. I placed my hand on his chest. His heart was racing. My medical knowledge extends to watching several seasons of *Grey's Anatomy*, so I'm not a medical expert by any means. But I knew at that moment he needed to see a doctor immediately. I loaded my sweet toddler into the car, grabbed my purse, and took him straight to the hospital by our home. I hoped the ER doctor would tell me I was overreacting and send us right back home.

Boy, was I wrong.

After multiple blood draws and one inconclusive ultrasound, James and I were granted a ride on an ambulance to the Children's Hospital in Dallas. We arrived at 4:00 a.m., and by this time my sweet boy seemed lifeless and couldn't even sit up. The doctor ordered James a CT scan. The results were terrifying.

Not only did he have appendicitis, but his appendix had ruptured. James had developed peritonitis, which means his entire belly was filled with infected fluid from his ruptured appendix. Peritonitis can be very serious and can even cause death if not treated right away. His intestines and some organs not only slowed but had completely stopped working. They were frozen and in shock from the infection filling his abdomen.

I was laying in the hospital bed next to him when the nurses rushed into the room and declared that he needed to go into surgery *immediately*. I asked if we could wait for my husband to arrive.

"No. The surgeon needs to operate NOW. We cannot wait."

Two nurses swiftly lifted James's small and unmoving body onto a gurney and quickly wheeled him toward the elevator. It was at that moment I realized just how serious of a situation this was. I ran to catch up with the nurses and held James's hand as he entered the pre-op room.

My husband, Matt, arrived and we were taken to an empty waiting room. Time stood still. I don't know how many minutes or hours had passed, but I felt like we were waiting a lifetime to hear from the pediatric surgeon. We prayed for a successful surgery and hoped for good news.

Eventually, the doctor walked into the room and took a seat across from us. I'll never forget the look on his face. He leaned forward and rested his elbows on his knees. With both hands clasped together, he looked straight into our eyes and told us that our son was in critical condition.

Years later, I can only remember fragments of what he said that day.

> . . .*very concerning. . .currently in the ICU. . .*
> . . .*couldn't get all the infection. . .*
> . . .*organs in shock. . .*

We were led to the ICU, where James was sleeping, fighting the infection in his body. The doctors were worried about his blood becoming septic, which can be life-threatening as well.

Thankfully, the antibiotics they had given him to fight off the infection did their job. The aftermath of his surgery and infection were incredibly miserable. James was on pain medicine around the clock and couldn't eat or drink anything. He had a feeding tube in his nose. IVs and wires surrounded his body. Slowly, James healed and became stronger over the next week.

The surgeon was very concerned for James. He told us we would be in the hospital for a minimum of three weeks. Our three-year-old son had hundreds (if not thousands) of people praying for him during this time. To the doctor's surprise, we walked out of the hospital seven days later with a prescription for antibiotics and a follow-up appointment scheduled.

I'm extremely thankful I was able to focus on our son during those tiring and stressful days instead of the bills that were certainly piling up. By this time, we were debt free and had about $15,000 in our savings account to cover any emergencies.

Our emergency fund brought us peace of mind during this stressful time. We didn't know if we would be able to pay for all our medical bills, but I knew our savings account would help cover some of the cost of this entire experience.

Emergencies happen. It's not a matter of *if* they will happen but *when* emergencies will happen. While we can't tell the future, we can do our best to prepare for whatever life throws at us. It all starts with having an emergency fund in place.

Why Have an Emergency Fund?

Dealing with my son's appendix crisis was a huge emergency, both on an emotional and financial level. Many emergencies are smaller, but you still need to be ready for them. Emergencies can include car or home repairs, sudden changes in your income level, unexpected litigation, or any of a range of events. Even something that seems like a relatively minor, everyday event can quickly turn into an emergency, as happened with our dog Joey.

While my husband and I were working to pay off $111,000 of debt, our dog at the time jumped a chain link fence and injured his foot. Matt immediately took him to an emergency vet. Little did we know, the vet wrapped Joey's leg too tight and didn't prescribe him a strong enough antibiotic to fight off infection.

Days later we removed Joey's bandages and noticed that his leg looked dull and lifeless. We took him to our personal vet and learned that Joey had developed a terrible case of gangrene in his leg. Essentially, his leg was dead, and the gangrene was creeping up his body. If we wanted to save Joey's life, he would need his leg amputated as soon as possible. At that time, we had $4,000 in our emergency fund. The vet told us his surgery would cost about $3,000 total.

This surgery was a shock to our family, but we were incredibly grateful that we had money in an emergency fund to cover the cost. We didn't have to go into debt to save his life. We didn't have to take four steps back when it came to our money goals. Instead, we were able to focus on helping our sweet "tripawd" (a three-legged dog) get better!

Our emergency fund served us with our dog Joey just as it did with our son, James.

Your emergency fund has one sole purpose: to help cover any unexpected expenses so you don't have to go into debt to pay for them. As you're working to become debt free and manage your money better, the *last* thing you want to do is go into debt when an emergency arises.

That's why setting up an emergency fund is imperative to your financial health. Emergencies catch us off guard, can cause us to go into more debt, and increase the stress in our life. By setting up an emergency fund for your family, you're taking a proactive approach to facing life's unexpected expenses head on.

What Your Emergency Fund Should Cover

I once tried to convince my husband to take me on a beach vacation using our emergency fund. I was desperate for some sun and ocean waves. As a teacher with summers off, it was difficult to scroll social media and witness everyone else enjoying the wonderful vacations that I longed for. My husband was teaching summer school, but I knew we could swing a four-night trip. I had calculated the cost, and we had *just enough* money to pay for the entire trip if we used our emergency fund.

Thankfully, my husband stood strong and kindly reminded me that beach vacations are *not* actual emergencies. *Darn!*

Over the years, my husband and I have used our emergency fund for *many* things including surgery for my son (twice!), vet visits, a new transmission for my husband's car, plumbing issues in our home, and plenty of unexpected medical bills.

Over the years I've been *tempted* to use our emergency fund on countless vacations, new furniture, unnecessary home updates, and anything else that caught my eye.

Your emergency fund is for just that: *emergencies*. But what qualifies as an emergency? In the moment it can sometimes be hard to determine if the cost you are facing is a want or a need. Table 6.1 provides a breakdown of what you should and should not use your emergency fund for.

Table 6.1 Is It an Emergency?

Use Your Emergency Fund	Do NOT Use Your Emergency Fund
Surprise medical bills	Christmas or holiday gifts
Necessary home repairs	Vacations
Necessary car repairs	New technology or furniture
Expenses after job loss	Unnecessary home updates
Emergency pet expenses	Entertainment

It's important to have a clear picture of what your emergency fund will and will not cover. Come back to this list any time you're tempted to use your emergency fund.

How Much Should Be in Your Emergency Fund

Many people wonder *how much* money they should save in their emergency fund. The answer varies based on your current life experiences and current expenses.

A good goal is to save three months of *necessary* expenses in your emergency fund. We only include necessary expenses in your emergency fund because if needed, you can cut back on unnecessary expenses temporarily.

What qualifies as a necessary expense? While it might be tempting to include Netflix or your favorite subscription as a necessary expense, those likely won't make the cut.

Table 6.2 includes a list of expenses for the average household. This table lists which expenses are necessary and which expenses should not be included in your emergency fund. Of course, this isn't set in stone, so use your best judgment when you decide which expenses are necessary for you.

Table 6.2   Necessary vs. Unnecessary Expenses

Necessary Expenses	Unnecessary/Extra Expenses
Rent/mortgage	Restaurants
Groceries	Netflix
Utility bills (electricity, water, gas)	Streaming subscriptions
Internet	Entertainment/concerts
Cell phones	Gym memberships
Childcare or daycare	Haircare
Life insurance	Christmas savings
Car insurance	Technology upgrades
Car payment	
Gas (for cars)	
Minimum debt payments	

Once you've identified which expenses are necessary, it's time to calculate how much you'll need in your emergency fund.

How to Calculate Your Emergency Fund

Calculating your emergency fund can be simple and straightforward. Follow the steps below to find out how much money should be in your emergency fund.

1. List out all your monthly expenses and how much they cost;

2. Highlight the *necessary* expenses;

3. Add the necessary expenses together; and

4. Multiply the total number by three.

Table 6.3 provides an example of how one family would calculate how much money they should save for their emergency fund. Each expense listed would be considered a necessary expense. I even added therapy as a necessary expense in this case because I believe it's important to still prioritize mental health.

Table 6.3 Sample Emergency Fund

Necessary Expense	Amount
Mortgage	$2,300.00
Internet	$57.00
Cell phones	$153.00
Car insurance	$155.00
Life insurance	$54.00
Car payment (minimum payment)	$302.00
Student loan (minimum payment)	$296.00
Credit card (minimum payment)	$75.00
Electricity + gas	$230.00
Water	$60.00
Groceries	$600.00
Gasoline	$200.00
Therapy	$150.00
Total	**$4,632.00**

Now it's just a matter of grabbing a calculator and crunching a few numbers. Follow the formula below:

Necessary Expenses × **3 months** = **Emergency Fund**
$4,632.00 × 3 months = $13,896.00

This family has $4,632.00 each month of necessary expenses. That means they would need to save $13,896.00 for a three-month emergency fund.

A little shocking, right? I personally was taken aback the first time I saw our family's emergency goal number. That's a *lot* of money to save! It might even take you a while to save your emergency fund. But I can *promise* you that when you need the money, you'll be thankful to have your emergency fund cash sitting in savings to cover any expenses such as major car repairs, unexpected medical costs, or even a job loss.

Do you feel like you'll *never* be able to save three months of necessary expenses? That's totally normal. But you have to start *somewhere*. What if you set a goal to save half that amount? It's okay to start small and build your emergency fund up over time.

Now it's your turn! Download your own Emergency Fund Page at www.inspiredbudget.com/moneymadeeasy. List out your necessary expenses and calculate how much money you should save in your emergency fund.

Emergency Fund Page

Necessary Expense	Amount
	$
	$
	$
	$
	$
	$
	$
	$
	$
	$
	$
	$
	$
	$
	$
	$
	$
	$
	$
	$
	$
	$
	$
	$
	$
	$
	$
Total	**$**

Saving for Emergencies

Now, do the math!

$$\text{Necessary Expenses} \times 3 \text{ months} = \text{Emergency Fund}$$

$$\underline{\hspace{3cm}} \times 3 \text{ months} = \underline{\hspace{3cm}}$$

Perfect! This should give you a good idea of how much money you need to set aside in your emergency fund.

Where to Store Your Emergency Fund

Once you know how much money you want to set aside in your emergency fund, you might be wondering *where* you should keep this money. You might be tempted to let this money accrue in your checking account. I don't know about you, but if I have extra money in my checking account, I'm tempted to spend it.

Below are three options for where to save your emergency fund. Pick the system that works best for you.

Option A: Standard Savings Account

When my husband and I were first setting aside money in an emergency fund, we kept it in a simple savings account that was connected to our checking account. The benefit of storing your emergency fund in a regular savings account is that your money is easily accessible.

With a click of a button, we could transfer money over to our checking account to pay for our dog's emergency leg amputation. We didn't have to wait several business days to have access to our money. While standard savings accounts are notorious for having very low interest rates (meaning your money isn't earning you much at all), we kept our money there for convenience.

The benefit of keeping your money in a standard savings account all comes down to convenience: it's incredibly easy to access your money.

Option B: High-yield Savings Account

Another option is to keep your emergency fund in a high-yield savings account. **A high-yield savings account typically pays 20 times the average of a standard savings account.** This means that if you keep your money in a high-yield savings account, your money will *earn more money* compared to a standard savings account.

Online banks have made high-yield savings accounts easier to access than ever. Of course, high-yield savings accounts have their own downsides. Some have initial deposit requirements, minimum balance requirements, and some even have fees.

Another downside is that it typically takes a few days for you to transfer money from your high-yield savings account to your checking account and vice versa. This means it could take you a few business days to access your money. If you're faced with a true emergency, this could be frustrating. However, this extra hurdle could stop you from transferring money out of savings for something that wouldn't be qualified as a true emergency (like a beach vacation).

The benefit of keeping your money in a high-yield savings account is that you will earn more money in interest than a standard savings account. Will that growth outpace inflation? Most likely not! But it's still nice to have your money earn a little extra money.

Option C: Mix of Both

My personal favorite way to store my emergency fund includes a mix of both a standard savings account as well as a high-yield savings account. Our family currently keeps 50% of our emergency fund in a standard savings account and the other 50% in a high-yield savings account.

I've found that I like having easy access to a portion of my emergency fund *just in case* I need it. The other half is parked in a high-yield savings account where it can earn extra money in interest.

There is zero temptation to use that money because I know there's an extra hurdle to access it. This is a huge plus for a spender like me.

You can choose a percentage amount or dollar amount to keep in each savings account. Find what works for you and your family. Don't spend too long thinking this through. It's just a small detail in the overall picture of your finances. Make a decision, and move forward with it.

Where will you keep your emergency fund?

- Standard savings account;
- Online high-yield savings account; or
- Both.

You Used Your Emergency Fund. Now What?

In October 2021 our beloved dog Joey, passed away. We had been faced with a few emergency expenses the month before, so we were actively working to refill our emergency fund when he died.

Between the vet bills, biopsies, blood work, and cremation expenses, we were hit with more setbacks when it came to replenishing our emergency fund.

May I be real here? Sometimes emergencies and setbacks like this make me want to give up. I start to think, "Why bother trying? Something always goes wrong." But then I remind myself that while I can't predict what life will bring (including the expenses that come with it), I can do my best to set my family up for success.

So I did what I needed to do: I continued to focus on refilling my emergency fund once again. I told myself that I don't have to feel ashamed, guilty, or frustrated when I'm in a position to use my emergency fund. It's easy, and totally normal, to feel guilty for using money from your emergency fund. You've worked *hard* to save that money. When you end up using it to cover unexpected expenses, it can feel like a loss—literally.

But it only feels this way because you have money goals that you're working toward. When life happens, sometimes we have to put our goals on pause. This journey won't always go as planned—and it won't always look like how you pictured it would.

Instead of being frustrated or sad that you had to use your emergency fund to cover expenses, tell yourself that your money is doing what it needs to do at this moment. If you've built it up once, you can do it again.

Once you've used your emergency fund, the goal should be to replenish it as soon as you can. You can do this in several ways:

- Pause any *extra* payments to debt and send all extra money to your emergency fund;
- Sell any unused items around your home;
- Cut back on extra spending; and
- Make extra money.

The sooner you refill your emergency fund, the sooner you can work toward your other money goals!

What to Do When Your Emergency Fund Isn't Enough

Matt and I were two short months away from reaching our debt-free goal. We had been paying off debt for four years by this point. Four years of hard work, determination, and focus were paying off. We could see the light at the end of the tunnel.

I felt more empowered over my life and my money than I had ever felt before. It was during that month of our debt-free journey that we were handed another difficult situation.

It started out like every other doctor visit. The pediatrician was completing her standard checkup on my youngest son. He was

18 months old and appeared to be the picture of health. However, during that visit she lingered a little longer than usual. I held my breath—*something wasn't right.*

One week later my husband and I were driving into downtown Fort Worth to see one of the top pediatric surgeons in the area. He completed a few scans and gave us the news that James would need surgery in the next five months.

Five months. We had five full months to prepare and save for this necessary surgery. Insurance would cover a portion of the procedure, but we were still left with thousands of dollars to pay. There was no doubt in my mind that my husband and I would do whatever it took so that James could get the medical help he needed.

However, we did have a problem: we didn't have enough money in our emergency fund at the time to cover the scans, surgery, and hospital bills. Thankfully, we had some time on our side to find a solution before his scheduled surgery date.

For the next five months we did *everything* we could to save money. We stopped sending extra money to debt, cut back on extra spending, and I even earned extra money by teaching summer school. Every extra penny we had went into our savings account. The day of James's surgery we had enough money to cover the cost of his procedure. We went from not having enough money to having just enough.

You might find yourself in a similar situation one day. There could come a time when the amount of money you have saved in your emergency fund doesn't cover the unexpected expense that you're faced with. In this moment, you might feel defeated, but remember that you always have choices open to you. Sometimes we just need to dig a little to find them.

Steps to Take

When life's emergencies and unexpected expenses arise, it's best to have a plan in place for how to handle them. Here's a checklist for what you can do when your emergency fund doesn't cover the cost of your emergency.

- If possible, get a second opinion or quote. Do your research to get a fair price.

- Pause any extra debt payments. When emergencies arise, it's okay to only make the minimum payments on your debts so you can focus on covering your expenses. Save any extra money you can find.

- Cut back on spending. There will be seasons of sacrifice in your life, but they are just that: seasons. Cutting back on your spending even for just a season allows you to save more money for your emergency expense.

- Increase your income. If you can, find a way to make more money, even if it's just temporarily. You can do this by selling unused items around your home, taking on a side hustle, or requesting more hours at work. The extra money you make can go toward your emergency expenses or emergency fund.

- Negotiate your bill. Some doctor's offices and hospitals are willing to offer a discount if you pay in full. Ask for a discount, and negotiate your bill.

- If you have a medical emergency, many hospitals are willing to work with you to set up a no-interest payment plan. This way, you pay your bill over time but don't end up paying interest to the hospital.

- Hospitals also have financial assistance programs. Ask the billing department about them. If you qualify, this could save you hundreds, if not thousands.

If you're faced with an unexpected expense that costs more than the amount of money you have in your emergency fund, don't be discouraged. Do what you can to cover the cost and then refill your emergency fund as soon as possible.

Remember, your emergency fund safeguards your money and finances so that you can still work toward your money goals.

Action Items

- List out your necessary expenses.
- Calculate your three-month emergency fund goal using the following formula:

Necessary Expenses × 3 months = Emergency Fund Goal

- Choose where you will keep your emergency fund.
  - Option A: Standard savings account;
  - Option B: Online high-yield savings account; or
  - Option C: Mix of both.
- Open your savings account, and start saving money for your emergency fund.
- List out a few ways you can find or save money if your emergency fund doesn't cover the cost of your unexpected expense.

Chapter 7

Setting Up Sinking Funds

It was a hot, summer day in Texas. I found myself standing in the lobby of a car repair shop just miles from my apartment. In that moment, I wished I was *anywhere* but there. I felt as if I were standing in an unfamiliar world, one I didn't quite understand how to navigate.

> *Why wasn't I more prepared for this type of situation?*
> *Why hadn't I saved money for a possible car repair?*

I was just a year out of college and had no idea that saving money for car repairs was the adult thing to do.

I stood at the counter and handed over my debit card. Minutes earlier I had transferred every penny from my tiny savings account to cover the cost of my car repairs. I now had absolutely no money in savings and was driving a car that appeared to be falling apart.

That night, financial anxiety kept me up late. I knew deep down that if I was faced with another unexpected expense, I would not be able to cover the bill. Every credit card application I filled out had been rejected. I had no money, no savings, and no backup plan.

If I had a car repair sinking fund in place that summer day many years ago, my situation would have been an annoying inconvenience instead of a moment that led to sleepless nights and extra stress.

I wish I could tell you that the stress of that summer day forced me to change my spending habits. However, it wasn't until a few years later that I started using sinking funds to save money for the expected (and unexpected) events that life throws at you.

What Is a Sinking Fund?

A sinking fund is a strategic way to set aside money for upcoming events, payments, or unexpected costs. Sinking funds provide a savings solution so you're more comfortably prepared when an expense hits.

Essentially, sinking funds save your sanity. They help cover the cost of expenses that would otherwise throw you completely off budget. Ultimately, saving money in sinking funds helps you stay in control of your money so you're no longer waiting around for the next expense to catch you off guard.

It's impossible to anticipate every expense that might come your way. But you can anticipate the common expenses that you'll be faced with, such as changing your car oil or spending money on Christmas gifts.

When you set up a sinking fund, you will essentially save as much or as little money you need each month to cover a specific expense. The moment you're faced with that expense, you'll have money to cover the cost. This removes the burden of paying for that expense out of your normal budget. It can also help you stay out of debt when expenses arise.

I like to save for three different types of sinking funds:

1. Save for what you *know* will happen;
2. Save for what you *want* to happen; and
3. Save for what *might* happen.

Each type of sinking fund has a specific purpose in your life.

Sinking Funds: What You Know Will Happen

It's important to set aside money for what you *know* will happen such as holidays, birthdays, home costs, and more.

For instance, we all know that Christmas falls on December 25th. And yet, many families go into debt each Christmas because they failed to set aside money to cover the cost of gifts, holiday activities, and new decorations. This leaves families stressed and overwhelmed financially each December because they didn't save money in advance. This financial stress can also have an impact on your peace of mind during what is supposed to be a wonderful time of the year.

Instead of facing the same money stress each December, consider setting up a sinking fund to cover the cost of Christmas. It's incredibly simple: transfer money into a separate savings account every month so that by the time December rolls around, you already have money set aside to pay for all your holiday expenses.

Another sinking fund our family has in place is to cover our yearly $1,100 homeowners association (HOA) dues. The bill appears in our mail each year during the same month. However, the first year of living in our home, we didn't have a sinking fund set up for these dues. Instead, we had to pull money from our emergency fund to cover the bill. Immediately after that experience we set up a sinking fund for our HOA dues. Each month we save money in a separate savings account. When our HOA bill arrives in the mail, all we need to do is transfer the money to our checking account and pay the bill.

Sinking funds are perfect for preparing for life events that you know are happening in advance such as:

- Holidays;
- Birthdays;

- Anniversaries;

- HOA dues;

- Home insurance (if paid yearly);

- Car insurance (if paid yearly or biyearly);

- Extracurricular events for kids;

- Back-to-school shopping.

You don't have to save for *every* expense that you know will happen, but it's a great idea to pick a few expenses that you can set up a sinking fund for.

Take a moment to use the Sinking Funds: What I Know Will Happen Worksheet to list out any sinking funds that you would like to include in your budget that you *know* will happen in your life. You can also download a free PDF version of this worksheet at www.inspiredbudget.com/moneymadeeasy.

Sinking Funds: What I Know Will Happen

Expenses I Know Will Happen	Goal Amount to Save
Total	$

Your future self will be thankful that you set aside money in sinking funds when these expenses arise.

Sinking Funds: What You Want to Happen

My favorite type of sinking fund is one that you save for expenses you *want* to happen in the future.

If you know that your family is going to take a beach trip this summer, then set up a sinking fund for the trip and start saving for your vacation in advance. Start by determining how much money your family will need for your trip, and calculate how much you'll need to save in your sinking fund each month to reach that goal. This way when it is time to enjoy fun in the sun, you have zero guilt for spending money.

When you are able to save for the expenses you *want* to happen in advance, you are actively taking control of your future and not letting your finances stand in the way of what you want to do. Plus, you'll have zero guilt or regrets when you can pay for what you want in cash.

I've included a few personal examples of how our family has set up sinking funds to pay for what we want to happen in life:

- Family vacations;
- Couple vacations;
- Summer camp for our kids;
- Home updates, such as new kitchen cabinets;
- Landscaping updates;
- A new car;
- New furniture.

Use the Sinking Funds: What I Want To Happen Worksheet to list out the sinking funds that you would like to save for. You can also download a free PDF version of this worksheet at www.inspiredbudget.com/moneymadeeasy.

Sinking Funds: What I Want To Happen

Expenses I Want To Happen	Goal Amount to Save
Total	$

These are the types of sinking funds that are exciting to save for once you are debt free and have extra money each month.

Sinking Funds: What Might Happen

The last type of sinking fund that you should consider adding to your budget is for expenses that *might* happen.

If you own a car, then setting aside money in a car maintenance sinking fund is a good idea. Chances are there will come a time when you find yourself standing in a car repair shop being told that you need new tires, or even worse, a new transmission. Setting aside money for car maintenance not only helps you cover the bill, but it eases the stress and anxiety that comes from larger repair bills.

Our family personally sets aside $50 each month for car maintenance. Years ago, my husband had to have his car transmission completely rebuilt. This was a shock to our finances. While the sinking fund we had in place did not cover the entire cost of his car repair, it did help cover part of the cost, which in turn lessened our overall stress.

Below is a list of possible sinking funds for events that *might* happen:

- Car maintenance/car repairs;
- Home maintenance;
- Emergency veterinary visits.

We can't always pinpoint *when* these unexpected expenses will happen. Yet when you have some money set aside to cover the cost of these expenses, it gives you a little more confidence, peace, and clarity when it comes to your money. This allows you to not feel stressed or overwhelmed when life happens. I don't know about you, but the less stressed I am about my finances, the more peace of mind I have.

Use the Sinking Funds: What Might Happen Worksheet to list sinking funds for expenses that *might* happen in your life. You can also download a free PDF version of this worksheet at www.inspiredbudget.com/moneymadeeasy.

Sinking Funds: What Might Happen

Expenses That Might Happen	Goal Amount to Save
Total	$

Great! Now it's time to get into the details of how sinking funds work as well as how to determine how much you should save in your sinking funds.

How Sinking Funds Work

Sinking funds start with a budget. You need to have a budget in place *before* you add sinking funds to your life. Think of your budget as the foundation to your money. Without your budget, you won't know how much money you can realistically contribute to each sinking fund every month. Once you have a budget in place, contributing to sinking funds is very simple.

When you sit down to write your budget, add each sinking fund as a line item in your budget. Just like you'd include electricity or Internet in your budget, make sure your sinking funds are a priority as well.

I personally save for sinking funds once a month because success with money comes from consistency. **When you contribute to sinking funds consistently, it becomes a positive money habit in your life.** You will no longer question whether saving money is important, and instead saving money becomes a nonnegotiable habit in your life.

When you're ready to spend the money in your sinking fund, simply transfer the money out of your savings account and use it.

How Much Money to Save

Once you know which sinking funds you want to include in your savings plan, it's time to determine *how* much money you want to save for each sinking fund.

Let's say you want to spend $1,200 for Christmas. This should include both Christmas gifts and every other Christmas-related expense (such as pictures with Santa and holiday decor). Take the amount you want to save and divide it by the number of months you have until you plan to spend the money.

Goal amount ÷ number of months = amount to save each month.

If you want to save $1,200 for Christmas and you start saving in January, then you'll take $1,200 and divide it by 12 months.

$$\$1,200 \div 12 \text{ months} = \$100 \text{ each month.}$$

That comes out to $100 each month, which means you'll want to set aside $100 each month into a separate savings account.

But what if you didn't start saving money in January? Let's say you start saving in June, which is only six months away from Christmas. Now, the equation looks a little different.

$$\$1,200 \div 6 \text{ months} = \$200 \text{ each month.}$$

Instead of only saving $100 each month, you need to save $200 each month to reach your goal. Moral of the story: give yourself a longer runway when it comes to saving money. The sooner you save for yearly events like this, the less money you need to set aside each month.

Now it's your turn! You have already brainstormed which sinking funds you want to include in your budget as well as how much you want to save for each sinking fund. Complete the Sinking Funds: How Much to Save Worksheet to determine how much money you need to save each month to reach your goal. You can also download this worksheet at www.inspiredbudget.com/moneymadeeasy.

Sinking Funds: How Much to Save

Sinking Fund Name	Goal Amount	÷	Number of Months	=	Amount to Save Each Month
Example: Back-to-school supplies and clothes	*$400.00*	÷	*5*	=	*$80*
		÷		=	
		÷		=	
		÷		=	
		÷		=	
		÷		=	
		÷		=	
		÷		=	
		÷		=	
		÷		=	
		÷		=	
		÷		=	
		÷		=	
		÷		=	
		÷		=	
		÷		=	
		÷		=	
		÷		=	
		÷		=	

Not every sinking fund needs to start with the end in mind. There might be some sinking funds, such as car maintenance, that you choose to contribute to each month without a "goal amount" that you're trying to reach. This is exactly what our family does.

When it comes to saving for sinking funds, it's important to find ways to make saving money an easy part of your routine. For instance, all cars need to be replaced eventually. If you have a car loan, continue paying it off. Once you make your last payment, continue paying the same amount each month but moving forward, send the money to a "New car" sinking fund. Because you're already comfortable with the monthly payment, this shouldn't be a major shock to your budget. When it comes time to buy the next car, you can use the money you saved toward the down payment, which lowers your monthly payments on your new car. If you're a married couple with two cars, this comes in handy.

Adding Sinking Funds to Your Budget

You might be wondering how many sinking funds you actually *need* in your life. The idea of saving for ten or more sinking funds can feel overwhelming. Plus, you might not have enough money each month to contribute to every sinking fund if you're also trying to pay off debt.

Instead of letting that get the best of you, consider starting off with just one or two important sinking funds right now. I recommend choosing two areas of your life that cause you the most stress.

If thinking about paying for unexpected dental work causes you stress and anxiety, then set up a dental sinking fund. If your car is constantly breaking down and you're hit with unexpected car repairs often, then set up a car maintenance sinking fund.

Focusing on one or two essential sinking funds allows you to reach your other money goals while becoming familiar with how sinking funds can save your financial sanity.

Now it's your turn.

- What are one or two areas of your finances that cause you stress and anxiety?

- Which areas of your spending would you love to have a little extra money set aside so that when an expense hits, you're prepared to cover the cost?
- Which area of your money frustrates you the most?

Where to Keep Sinking Funds

One of the questions I receive often is "*Where should I keep my sinking funds?*"

You have three basic options when it comes to where you stash your sinking funds. The good news is that you can choose whichever method works best for you. You also have the freedom to change where you keep your sinking funds as time goes on.

Option 1: Cash

A great way to organize your sinking funds is to pull the money out of your bank and keep your sinking funds in cash. If you know that you'll struggle with using money that's linked to your savings account for another purpose, then cash envelopes might be a great place to keep your sinking funds.

This is the perfect solution for those sinking funds that you might need to "grab and go" such as your car maintenance sinking fund.

As someone who personally struggles with overspending on a debit card or credit card easily, I like using cash envelopes for some of my sinking funds because I tend to show more restraint when spending cash. Our family currently keeps our car maintenance sinking fund and clothing sinking fund in cash. This way, if we need to buy our son new shoes, we can quickly grab the clothing sinking fund envelope and head to the shoe store. It also helps our children know exactly what their budget is when it comes to shopping for shoes. They can see exactly how much money we can spend!

Of course, there are some pros and cons when it comes to keeping your sinking funds in cash. See Table 7.1.

Table 7.1 Keeping Sinking Funds in Cash

Pros	Cons
• Cash is easy to access and readily available. • Cash is usually harder to spend than a debit card or credit card.	• Your cash won't earn any money as it would in a traditional or high-yield savings account. • Cash can be easily misplaced. Have a specific spot where you keep your cash in sinking funds.

Cash envelopes are a great place for keeping sinking funds that won't add up to thousands of dollars in savings. I don't know about you, but I personally don't like keeping a lot of cash on hand at home. However, the sinking funds I do save in cash don't tend to add up to a lot of money.

Option 2: Standard Savings Account

The second option for storing your sinking funds is to set up a savings account for each sinking fund that is linked to your main checking account. This way, the money is still easy to access and can be transferred over to your checking account with the click of a button.

Many banks will allow you to open multiple savings accounts. You might even be able to rename your savings accounts to match your sinking fund. For instance, our family has an HOA Dues sinking fund that we keep in a standard savings account at our bank. This way when we pay our yearly HOA dues, we can make one transfer out of our sinking fund into our checking account and pay the dues online.

See Table 7.2 for a quick overview of the pros and cons of keeping sinking funds in savings accounts.

Table 7.2 Keeping Sinking Funds in Saving Accounts

Pros	Cons
• A standard savings account connected to your checking account is easy to access. • Your money is safe and has a place when it lives in its own dedicated savings account.	• If you're tempted to move money from savings to pay for other expenses, this could possibly hinder your sinking funds goals.

We personally have two sinking funds that are connected to our standard checking account. I love that the money is easy to access but not sitting inside our home.

Option 3: Online High-yield Savings Account

By far my favorite option for keeping your sinking funds safe is to set up a high-yield savings account online. This type of account tends to pay out a higher interest rate than traditional savings accounts. While you likely won't become rich by keeping your sinking funds in a high-yield savings account, you will at least earn *some* money for keeping your sinking funds here.

Many online high-yield savings accounts are completely free. Some don't have a minimum balance requirement or an initial deposit requirement. This means you can have as much, or as little, money in your online high-yield savings account as you'd like.

To transfer money to an online saving account, you'll need to link your current checking account to the savings account. The only downside is that it typically takes two or three business days for the money to transfer over completely. This means that if you have an emergency, you won't necessarily be able to access your money right away.

Table 7.3 Keeping Sinking Funds in High-yield Savings Accounts

Pros	Cons
• Online high-yield savings accounts have higher interest rates, meaning your money will earn more money compared to standard savings accounts. • Your money is difficult to reach (it takes a few days to access your money), which means you'll be less likely to spend it on something else.	• Your money is difficult to reach (it takes a few days to access your money). If you need access to your money right away, you will likely have to wait a few days.

I personally keep our Christmas sinking fund and vacation sinking fund in an online high-yield savings account because I don't anticipate needing my money any time soon for those expenses. When I do need to spend the money I've saved, I should know well enough in advance. This way, it's not a headache when it takes a few business days for my money to transfer back into my checking account.

Just like any other option, an online high-yield savings account has its pros and cons, as you can see in Table 7.3.

Choosing Your Sinking Fund Locations

The best part about choosing where to keep your sinking funds is that you can choose several options to find what works for you. You can keep one sinking fund in cash, a few in a standard savings account, and one in an online high-yield savings account. Ultimately, the goal is to make sinking funds work for you, so mix and match as you wish.

Take a moment to decide where you want to keep your sinking funds. Each sinking fund can have its own location. Use the Sinking Funds Location Worksheet to list out the sinking funds you'd like to include in your budget, and check off where you want to keep them. You can also download a free PDF version of this worksheet at www.inspiredbudget.com/moneymadeeasy.

Sinking Funds Location

Sinking Fund Name	Location		
	Cash Envelope	Standard Savings Account	Online High-yield Savings Account
Example: *Vacation fund*			✓

You've Used Your Sinking Funds. Now What?

Using your sinking funds can feel both exhilarating and frustrating. On one hand, you are prepared for life's expected or unexpected expenses, which feels *amazing*. Look at you—you're getting this adulting thing down!

On the other hand, the money that you have diligently been setting aside is suddenly gone. Don't let the frustration you're feeling take away from the joy of being prepared when it comes to facing unexpected (or expected) expenses.

When you end up using your sinking fund money, it's time to decide whether you want to replenish your savings right away or whether you'd rather wait a few months to start saving in your sinking funds again. For instance, if I had to empty my car maintenance sinking fund for new tires, I would continue to replenish my sinking fund immediately. However, if I had to empty my vacation sinking fund, I might wait a few months after taking our vacation to start saving up for our next family trip.

No matter what you decide to do, it's important to remember that saving money in sinking funds will ultimately set you up for success in the future. I fully believe that your future self will be incredibly thankful that you saved money for holidays come December. Your future self will be glad that you had money in a car maintenance sinking fund when it comes time to replace your tires.

It's a wonderful feeling to know that what you're doing *now* will have an impact on your life later. Don't skip on sinking funds. They ultimately lead to peace of mind, less stress, and give you a clear mind when you're faced with life's expected and unexpected expenses.

Action Items

- Determine which types of sinking funds you want to add to your budget. There are three types of sinking funds you might want to include:

  - Save for what you *know* will happen;

  - Save for what you *want* to happen; and

  - Save for what *might* happen.

- If you're new to sinking funds, choose only one or two sinking funds to add to your budget. Answer the following questions to help you determine which sinking funds you should start with first:

  - What are one or two areas of your finances that cause you stress and anxiety?

  - Which areas of your spending would you love to have a little extra money set aside for so that when an expense hits, you're prepared to cover the cost?

  - Which area of your money frustrates you the most?

- Use the following equation to determine how much money you need to save each month to reach your sinking fund goal:

Goal amount ÷ number of months = amount to save each month.

- Choose where you will keep each sinking fund. Options include:

  - Cash envelope;

  - Standard savings account; and

  - Online high-yield savings account.

Chapter 8

Goal Setting: The Ultimate Game Changer

I'm what my husband likes to call a "dreamer." I have amazing, incredible views of what my life will look like and what I will accomplish. Usually, these dreams seem completely off the wall to my husband, who tends to be more realistic. For instance, I have been known to spend hours on end researching how much a mountain home would cost in the heart of Colorado. I'll happily spend my free time on Zillow browsing cabins, tiny homes, and luxurious escapes, dreaming about what it would be like to have a summer home in the mountains. *Like I said, I'm a dreamer!*

The only problem with my grand dreams? I have a track record of *only* dreaming and not *doing*. In the past I would spend most of my energy thinking about what I wanted my life to look like and never actually take any action to get there.

This unfortunate habit had a few unintentional consequences:

1. My husband no longer took my dreams or aspirations seriously. *Why should he when I never followed through on them?*

2. I started to doubt myself and my ability to reach these sometimes over-the-top goals. *Could I do these things, or is my head just stuck in the clouds?*

Then one day I decided that I was *done* dreaming.

I was *done* thinking about everything I wanted to do but had never taken action on in the past.

I was ready to act. I was ready to *do* instead of *dream*. That's the day I started setting goals for my money, my family, and my life.

Deep down, I realized that no one was going to hold me by the hand and help me reach my dreams. Not to mention, I tend to lose focus on what I need to do to get to where I want to be. Goal setting would be the solution to my problem.

Setting goals became the thing I did to create a plan for what I wanted in my life. I started setting goals for my money, my family, my home, and my health. Admittedly, I became a little obsessed and over the top when it came to setting goals. *Why?* Because nothing else had ever worked in the past.

Once I started setting goals, I was no longer wishing, and instead I was doing. I could easily break my big goals down into smaller, actionable steps. This was very freeing for me. Not only did I start to develop confidence in myself and my ability to reach my goals, but my husband no longer doubted what I was capable of. For years I never followed through. But now, he knows that I can (usually) accomplish my goals if I can focus my energy.

I was seeing results from my efforts for the first time in my life. Instead of spending all my time dreaming about what life *could* look like, I was taking steps in the right direction to make my dreams a reality. And while we might not have our mountain home *yet*, I know that it's not just a dream—it's a goal that I could possibly one day reach.

One of my *favorite* areas to set goals for is our money. The benefits of setting financial goals are worth the time and effort it takes.

The Benefits You Can't Ignore

There are likely thousands of published books explaining the *best* way to set goals and reach them. Why are there so many people willing to write about goal setting? *Because it works.*

Not only does setting goals for your money help you get to where you want to be, but it comes with several benefits that you simply cannot ignore.

Benefit #1: You Have a Clear Path to Follow

When Matt and I first decided to pay off over $111,000 of debt, the idea felt nearly impossible. I sat in shock thinking it couldn't be done. Meanwhile, Matt grabbed a calculator and started doing the math.

He took our large goal of paying off all our debt and divided it by five years.

$$\$111,000 \div 5 \text{ years} = \$22,200 \text{ each year.}$$

If we wanted to pay off all our debt in five years, we would have to pay off $22,200 each year. Then, Matt took this amount and divided it by 12 months.

$$\$22,200 \div 12 \text{ months} = \$1,850 \text{ each month.}$$

Within just a few minutes we had a plan. If we wanted to reach our big goal of becoming debt free, we knew about how much money we would need to send to debt each year and each month.

These simple calculations were our first taste of setting goals for our money. The benefit couldn't be ignored: we now had a clear path to follow. **The idea of paying off debt was no longer intimidating because we broke it down into manageable pieces.**

When you're willing to break down your money goals into actionable steps, you will realize that all you're doing is creating your own path, or plan, to follow. Reaching your goals suddenly becomes *easier* because you don't have to spend any mental energy trying to figure out *how* to get to your end goal. Instead, you just need to follow the steps you set.

Benefit #2: Your Communication Improves

Money is a touchy subject, especially when you share money with a significant other. Each person has their own vision for how money should be spent and saved. The thought of aligning your expectations with your partner's might feel similar to completing a 1,000-piece puzzle while blindfolded. However, if you're *not* talking about money, then it's nearly impossible to align your expectations and get on the same page.

Setting money goals together gives you the opportunity to communicate about your finances and not just get on the same page about money but stay on the same page as well. This is exactly what happened for me and my husband.

As someone who is often tempted to spend money very easily, there have been several times when I'm about to buy an item only to pause and think, "Wait. Matt and I just talked about our money goals and what we want to accomplish. Does this purchase support that goal?" This is *huge* for someone like me. To pause mid-scroll on Amazon takes the type of willpower that I never thought I would embody. And it all started with sitting down with my spouse, communicating openly about money, and setting goals for our finances.

Benefit #3: You're More Likely to Follow through with Your Goals

One January I decided that I would be a better mom, wife, and employee if I started waking up at 5:00 a.m. *Why?* Because everyone says that the earlier you wake up, the more productive you are. I listed out everything I could accomplish in the early morning hours. I could pray and read a devotional. I could go running or exercise. Maybe I could even do a little housework before everyone woke up.

My intentions were wonderful and genuine, but my follow-through was flawed. I started by diving straight into my new and improved morning routine. My alarm went off at 5:00 a.m., and I hopped out of bed. My only problem? I had failed to go to bed an hour earlier the night before.

For two weeks I did my best to function on less sleep than normal. And then it happened: my body said, "NO MORE." I crashed. After fourteen days I gave up and went back to sleeping in until 6:30 a.m. Instead of creating a plan to wake up earlier, such as moving my wake-up time ahead in fifteen-minute increments, I jumped in with two feet and failed to create a plan that would make my goal attainable.

Are you guilty of making the same mistake I did?

Have you ever set a goal for the new year only to give up by January 14th? Maybe you were determined to pay off debt or start budgeting so you could save money. But within two months you decided that it was just too complicated or wouldn't work for you. It's easy to become overwhelmed when you're standing before a massive goal that feels impossible to accomplish.

Setting money goals and breaking them down into smaller steps allows you to make progress the entire year, not just during the first two months. Instead, you'll stay focused and know what steps you need to take all year long.

Most importantly, setting realistic and actionable goals for your money gives you the ability to turn what would have been a failed New Year's resolution into your reality.

Benefit #4: Your Children See Goal Setting in Action

If you're a parent, then you likely want to give your children the world. We want our children to be happy, healthy, and safe. Unfortunately, the world tells us that to keep our kids happy, we must buy them more *stuff*. More toys. More technology. More clothes. More of everything.

Conversely, what our kids *really* need is the opportunity to watch their parents' set goals and manage their money with confidence. They need to see what it looks like to live on less than you make and practice responsible spending. Our kids need to see what it looks like to pay off debt and save for the future. And most of all, they need to see what it looks like to say, "No" or "Not right now" to what doesn't serve you financially.

Setting goals for your money and letting your children *see* what that process looks like will have a major impact on their lives. You're giving them a front row seat to learning what it looks like to work for a financial goal and what to do when unexpected expenses arise.

This benefit to setting money goals was completely unexpected for our family. We didn't realize that communicating out loud what we wanted for our money would have such an impact on our own children. We didn't realize how much they would pick up and in turn be able to apply to their own life.

When you set money goals, your children are watching. They are learning, through your own progress, how to set and reach goals of their own. What an amazing benefit of goal setting that has an impact on the entire family. This is even true if your children are already fully grown and living on their own. It also sets a great example for retired parents, other family, friends, neighbors, and members of the community.

How to Set Money Goals

We all know that setting goals in life is important, but so many people ignore this fact and skip goal setting completely. It's not that people want to fail or accomplish less, it's that they never learned how to properly set goals.

People who set specific, measurable goals are more likely to reach success. The best way to set and reach your goals is to start with the end in mind and work your way back from there. Below are the exact steps that our family, and many others that I teach, take each year to review past goals as well as set new, realistic goals.

Step 1: Review and Reflect

Before you dive into setting new goals for yourself, it's important to take a moment to reflect on your past habits, patterns, and financial truth. Be honest with how the past year has looked for you and your money. Reflecting on your past money choices will allow you to set realistic goals for your future.

Start by answering the questions below about the past year:

- What has changed or affected your money in the past year?
- How are you different now than you were a year ago?

- How has your view of money or finances changed?

- When it comes to your money, what are you proud of from last year?

- What challenges have you faced with your money?

- What needs to change in your life when it comes to your money?

- What are you willing to leave behind, and what are you willing to bring with you this year?

For example, years ago I fell into the same pattern every night: I would put my kids to bed, plop down on the sofa downstairs, and open the Amazon app while I watched a Netflix show.

I would browse Amazon's suggestions for what they thought would bring me joy, and without even giving it a second thought, I'd click "Add to cart." Over time I realized that I needed to leave behind mindless online shopping and instead focus on spending money intentionally and with purpose.

What money habits do you need to leave behind? Don't ignore this step. It's the foundation for creating goals that are realistic and true to you.

Step 2: Set Your Intentions

Now that you've reflected on your financial past, you're ready to set intentional money goals for your future. It's important to take into consideration where you are *starting*, which is why you reflected on your past money experiences.

It's time to be intentional and think about what you *want* to achieve. Take a moment to write everything you'd like to do with your money down on a piece of paper. Don't hold anything back in this step. Write down what you'd like to accomplish this month, this year, or even in the next ten years. No goal or thought should be left unturned. Write it all down, even if you feel like you won't be able to achieve it. I've found that when I write out a goal, even the big ones, they start to feel less like a dream and more like an opportunity.

Once you have listed all your goals and dreams on a piece of paper, it's time to ask yourself whether you're willing to accept the sacrifices that might come along with this goal.

When I was in the early years of building my business, Inspired Budget, I was a wife, mom of two, and a full-time teacher. My time was limited. And yet, I had the goal to create a business that would replace my teaching income and let me work from home full-time. I *knew* that there would be sacrifices I would have to make if I wanted to reach this goal. There simply wasn't enough time in my day to do it all, so something had to give. I ultimately decided that I was willing to accept the trade-offs that came with reaching my goal. Within two years I was able to leave teaching and work on Inspired Budget full time.

There's no doubt about it: we must make sacrifices when it comes to reaching our goals. The ultimate question is whether you're willing to accept those sacrifices. The answer is a simple yes or no. It's okay if you don't want to accept the sacrifices that come with reaching your goal, but that means you must be willing to modify your goal to make it more reasonable and realistic.

For example, when my husband and I were paying off debt, we would set a yearly debt payoff goal. One year we set a goal to pay off $20,000 of debt. To reach this goal, we had to be willing to accept the sacrifices that came along with it. For us, this meant that we wouldn't be able to afford an elaborate family vacation. Instead, our family vacation would consist of visiting out-of-town family members

Goal Setting: The Ultimate Game Changer

and staying with them. At the time, we had young kids, and it was easy to accept this trade-off. We figured our kids wouldn't remember a grand vacation anyway, so it wasn't difficult for us to pass on a costly trip together. However, now that our kids are older and we are focusing on creating memories with them, it would be a more difficult trade-off to accept.

Now that you've thought through what you want to achieve, it's time to think through the trade-offs and sacrifices that you'll have to make to get there. Decide whether it's *worth* the sacrifices to you. Not every goal is worth the sacrifices that come along with achieving it, and that's okay.

Step 3: Create Your Goal

Now that you have an idea of what you want to achieve, it's time to clearly state your goal and determine *how* you will reach your goal. I prefer to always start with the end in mind.

Option 1: Think about your end goal and determine *how long* it will take you to reach that goal.

For instance, if your goal is to become debt free, start with the end in mind: the amount of debt you have. If you want to pay off $50,000 of debt and you know that you can send $2,000 to debt each month, all you need to do is complete a simple math problem:

$$\$50,000 \div \$2,000 \text{ each month} = 25 \text{ months}.$$

You now have a monthly goal *and* a timeline in place. If you send $2,000 to debt each month, you should be able to become debt free in about 25 months, which is just over two years.

Option 2: Another option is to start with your end goal and break it down into a *monthly goal* for yourself.

Let's look at the same example as above. If you have $50,000 of debt, you could ask yourself *how long* you want to take to pay off your debt. If you only want to take 1.5 years to become debt free, then you just need to solve a simple math problem to determine how much debt you'll have to pay off each month to reach that goal.

$$\$50,000 \div 18\, \text{months} = \$2,778\, \text{each month}.$$

Now ask yourself: are you willing to make the sacrifices that come along with sending $2,800 each month to debt? Is it realistic for you?

If the answer is *no*, then add more time to your goal. The equation now becomes:

$$\$50,000 \div 30\, \text{months} = \$1,667\, \text{each month}.$$

Continue to work through the numbers until you reach a calculation that is realistic for you and your family. The best goals are clear, specific, and time bound, meaning they have a deadline tied to them.

Step 4: Review and Track Your Goals

The purpose when it comes to goal setting is to write goals that are realistic and ones that you can, and want, to achieve. Now that you have a goal in mind, it's time to review it.

Complete the Review the Goal Worksheet to review money goals you've set. You can also download a free PDF version of this worksheet at www.inspiredbudget.com/moneymadeeasy.

Review the Goal

My goal:	
What do you want to achieve?	
What sacrifices will you have to make to reach that goal?	
Is your goal realistic? Will you be able to meet your goal?	
How much time will your goal take to reach (what is your deadline?)	

If you've found that your goal is not realistic or a goal that you don't even *want* to reach, then go back and change it. You are more likely to meet goals that you're excited about.

Following is an example of a personal money goal that our family had in the past:

Review the Goal Example

My goal: *Invest our Roth IRAs to the max (currently $6,000 per person each year).*	
What do you want to achieve?	*I want to max out my Roth IRA as well as my husband's Roth IRA. This comes out to $12,000 each year.*
What sacrifices will you have to make to reach that goal?	*If we invest $1,000 each month, this means that we will have that much less to spend in our lives. We will have to budget and make sure to prioritize this money for investments.*
Is your goal realistic? Will you be able to meet your goal?	*Yes, if we continue to write a budget and live within our means, we should be able to send $1,000 each month to our Roth IRAs.*
How much time will your goal take to reach (what is your deadline?)	*We can both invest $500 each month ($1,000 combined) and reach our goal in one year.*

I personally enjoy filling out this form because it forces a dreamer, like me, to be more specific and realistic when it comes to the goals that I set. I also love that it forces me to think through whether I really want to achieve the goal I have in mind. Sometimes, I find that the sacrifices I would have to make aren't worth the goal I had originally wanted!

How Often to Set Goals

Another package arrived at the front door. I tried my best to run and grab it before he noticed, but it was too late. My husband had beat me to it. Matt turned around with the classic Amazon box in hand.

"Another one?" he asked.

"Um, yeah" I mumbled as he rolled his eyes and placed the package in my hands.

There was no doubt about it—my late-night Amazon shopping had taken a turn for the worse.

It turns out we purchased 21 items from Amazon in 40 days. I don't know about you, but that is a lot for us. That's when I decided to set a goal to drastically lower the number of Amazon purchases I made over the next month.

These types of small monthly goals, like cutting back on online shopping or simply cooking dinner at home six nights each week, motivate me like none other. They also have a direct impact on our finances.

Yet these are just a *few* of the goals that I set when it comes to my money. There are many types of goals that you'll want to consider when focusing on the type of life you want to achieve.

Long-term Goals

Long-term goals are goals that you would love to accomplish in the next 10 or more years. These goals include all the big dreams you have for your future such as owning a home or a piece of land. One of my long-term goals is to be able to retire at the same time as my husband. Because my husband is a few years older than me, I need to start thinking about what we need to invest *now* to reach our retirement goal a few years earlier.

Long-term goals might seem like a million years away right now, but every small step you make today brings you just a little bit closer to these goals. Sure, it's impossible to predict the future. But who says we can't set goals for our future and do our best to make it our reality?

Take time to think through what you want your future to look like. When do you want to retire? Where do you want to live? What do you want your life to look like? Answering these questions will help you think through what type of long-term goals you want to set for your life and your family.

Yearly Goals

Back in 2014 I had the *amazing idea* that Matt and I should set yearly money goals together. While I enjoy this process, my husband isn't as eager to dive into goal setting as I am. That's when I decided that the best time to set yearly goals together was when he couldn't escape the conversation. Instead of bothering him with goal setting at home, I saved these conversations for when we were trapped in the car on a road trip to visit family over the holidays. I now had a block of time where he couldn't get away from our goal-setting conversation. As we drove, we would discuss our yearly goals. And yes, the kids would hear the entire conversation.

When we set yearly goals together, we focus on four specific areas of our life.

1. **Faith:** What do we need to do to improve our faith and connection with God?
2. **Family:** What do we want to accomplish as a family? How do we want to improve our marriage?
3. **Fitness and health:** What do we want to accomplish to become healthier overall? How can we improve our mental, emotional, and physical health this year?
4. **Finances:** What money goals do we have for our family?

We set these goals both individually and as a family. For instance, my husband and I will set our own goals when it comes to our fitness and health. However, when it comes to finances, we set goals together as a family.

It's important to look back at your long-term goals when setting yearly goals. Ultimately, you want your yearly goals to support your long-term goals.

Now it's your turn! Use the Yearly Goals Worksheet to list out your own yearly goals. Create as many or as few goals as you'd like. Feel free to change the categories to match your needs. You can also print the Yearly Goals Worksheet at www.inspiredbudget.com/moneymadeeasy.

Yearly Goals

Category	Goal
Faith	
Family	
Fitness/health	
Finances	
Other:	
Other:	

Your yearly goals act as a road map for you throughout the year. It's important to look at these yearly goals and ask yourself what you need to do *monthly* to make your goals your reality.

Monthly Goals

The difference between people who give up on their goals every year and the people who reach them can usually come down to one thing: *intention*.

Setting monthly goals allows you to be intentional with how you spend your money and your time. It encourages you to look back at your yearly goals and decide what you can do *this month* to get one step closer to your yearly goal.

For instance, if your goal is to save $10,000 in your emergency fund, then set a savings goal each month to help you get there. You can also set a goal to cook dinner at home a certain number of nights so you'll stay on budget when it comes to eating out. These simple actions have a direct impact on whether you do, or do not, meet your emergency fund goal.

Likewise, if one of your money goals is to start investing, a monthly goal could be to write a budget and add investing as a line item in your budget. Another possible monthly goal could be to sit down with someone from the HR department to discuss what they offer their employees in terms of retirement accounts. Both of these simple monthly goals (budgeting and meeting with HR) can have a direct impact on you starting your investing journey. They get you one step closer to your yearly and long-term money goals!

Don't overthink your monthly goals. Just sit down and list three or four things that you would like to do this month that will help you take one step closer to your yearly goals.

Weekly Goals

Setting monthly goals is helpful, but why stop there? I've found that setting weekly goals allows me to take small, intentional steps in the right direction when it comes to what I want to achieve.

Weekly goals, while seemingly small, can help you stay on track. They support your monthly goals, which support your yearly goals.

Being intentional every week doesn't have to be time consuming. Simply take a few minutes at the start of your week to think about three things you'd like to accomplish. These tasks can be spread across different areas of your life. For instance, I usually set an exercise goal, a money goal, and a food goal such as cook dinner at home five nights each week. I jot them down on a sticky note and keep it on my desk. That's it.

Setting weekly goals allows you to be more intentional about how you spend your days and time. They give you something to strive for, even if that goal is to write your budget, track your spending, or cook dinner at home Monday through Friday.

Money Goals to Consider

In 2012 my husband and I were laser-focused on paying off debt as quickly as we could. We knew that becoming debt free meant that we would free up extra money each month to spend on what we wanted, instead of sending all our extra money to loans. During those years, our goals mostly revolved around paying off debt and spending money mindfully.

These days, we are focused on other types of money goals such as retirement and savings goals. Matt and I do our best to make investing for retirement and saving for family vacations a priority each month.

As you move through different seasons of life, your money goals will change. Embrace the change! Below are four different types of money goals that you might want to consider setting for yourself and your family. Over the years our family has set goals in each of these areas.

1. **Debt payoff goals:** If you have debt, consider setting a goal for how much debt you want to pay off each year or each month. Another option is to set specific goals for each loan. For instance, you might set a goal to pay off your lowest credit card in the next two months. Once you reach that goal, set a new goal for your next debt.

2. **Savings goals:** Saving money is important. Whether you're saving money for your emergency fund, holidays, or a family vacation, goal setting can help you stay motivated.

3. **Retirement goals:** It's easy to tell yourself, "I'll save for retirement later" as you're setting money goals—*especially* when you're in your twenties or thirties. However, you don't want to ignore this goal. One thing is for sure: one day you'll want to stop working. Saving money *now* for retirement pays off in the future, literally.

4. **Spending goals:** If you are tempted to spend money without thinking, then add spending goals to your life. Spending goals help you stay focused on spending what you planned and not

going overboard with spending unnecessarily. These goals can look like choosing to have two no-spend days each week where you don't spend a penny, or boundaries for how much money you'll spend at your favorite store.

Goal setting can be the game changer and motivator that you didn't know you needed. Get started by choosing one or two goals that you want to set for yourself right now.

Tips to Reach Your Goals

There's no doubt about it: goal setting can get you to where you want to be with your money. However, it's up to you to follow through on your goals, which—let's be honest—isn't always easy. But don't worry, I have some tips to help you reach the goals you set.

Tip #1: Check In on Your Goals Often

When it comes to following through on longer goals, such as yearly or long-term goals, it's important to check in on your goals often. Many people set a goal in January and ignore it. They forget what they were originally working toward. This happens because they aren't taking the time and energy to review and check in on their goals.

Instead, set a date in your calendar to review the goals you set, and ask yourself if you are making progress toward that goal. I personally do this once a quarter. Take a moment to look back at the goal you set, and ask yourself these questions:

- *Am I on track to reach this goal?*
- *If not, why? Is my goal unrealistic?*
- *What am I committed to doing in the next three months to help me get closer to where I want to be?*

Simply coming back and checking in on your goals more often keeps them at the forefront of your mind.

Tip #2: Break Your Goals Down

If you're setting big goals, consider breaking them down into bite-sized pieces. For instance, if you want to save $4,000 over the next five months, break your larger goal down into a monthly goal. This means you would have a goal to save $800 each month. This feels a lot more doable when you break your goal down.

The same can be said for almost any goal. For me, I have a goal to finish writing this book before a certain date. I decided that the best way to tackle this task was to break my big goal (writing an entire book) down into bite-sized goals: chapters. Instead of focusing on writing an entire book, I focus on one chapter at time. This tip might seem simple, but it can have an incredible impact on how you see—and reach—your goals.

Tip #3: Celebrate Your Progress

As you're working toward paying off debt, saving, or investing, it's easy to focus on what you *want* instead of celebrating what you've accomplished. It's easy to ignore the progress you've made, both financially and when it comes to your new money habits. Yet ignoring your progress ultimately leads to burnout.

Take time to celebrate the progress that you have made while on your money journey. If you paid off a loan, acknowledge that accomplishment. If you closed out of the Amazon app while mindlessly browsing something you could buy, celebrate that success. It's important to not spend all your time dwelling on where you want to be and instead take moments out of your life to give yourself a pat on the back for your efforts.

These small, or large, celebrations can actually give you a renewed sense of motivation when it comes to meeting your money goals. Who knows—it might be just the thing you need to stay focused on your financial journey.

Action Items

- Reflect on your past money choices by answering the following questions:

  - *What has changed or affected your money in the past year?*

  - *How are you different now than you were a year ago?*

  - *How has your view of money or finances changed?*

  - *When it comes to your money, what are you proud of from last year?*

  - *What challenges have you faced with your money?*

  - *What needs to change in your life when it comes to your money?*

  - *What are you willing to leave behind, and what are you willing to bring with you this year?*

- Set several long-term goals;
- Set several yearly goals;
- Set several monthly goals;
- Set several weekly goals; and
- Choose a date to check in on your yearly and long-term goals. Add these dates to your calendar.

Chapter 9

Conquering Impulse Spending
with Intention

The glass doors slid open, and I stepped into the crisp, white store. Before my feet even touched the sleek floor, I was repeating the same phrase over and over in my mind.

I will not spend money.
I will not spend money.
I will not spend money.

I was with two friends, and we had stopped by Ulta, one of my favorite beauty stores. One of my friends needed to grab a few items, and the other was eager to shop as well.

I had full confidence that I'd stay strong until I walked down the nail polish aisle. Next was the eyeshadow area. One by one, I started picking items up. Little by little, the phrase I had been repeating disappeared.

I like to think that what came next was a shock to me, but it had happened time and time again. I stood at the counter with my stomach in knots as the lady behind the register rang up each item. Here I was, spending money that I didn't have and didn't intend to spend.

I handed over my credit card as a wave of contrasting emotions settled in. Excitement for my new beauty items coupled with guilt because I didn't have the money to pay for them. I pushed all the negative emotions aside and walked out the door with my purchases in hand.

My friends had no clue I was fighting an internal battle, all within the past 25 minutes.

If you've experienced similar emotions while walking through a store or shopping online, then you're in the right place. The good news is that you can make amazing progress to combat impulse spending (I'm speaking from experience here!).

However, the work that it takes to stop impulse spending is deeper than simply unsubscribing from store emails. It looks like dealing with the deeper issues at hand and the real reasons behind your spending. When you can face those issues, you can combat impulse spending for good.

Impulse Spending: What Is it?

Years of impulse spending had a massive impact on my relationship with money. Because I spent money so often without thinking, I started to have guilt *any time* I swiped my debit card, even if it was for a planned expense such as groceries. You might, like I did, need to learn how to reframe your mind around one very important fact: **Spending money isn't "good" or "bad." Spending money is neutral.**

You'll have to spend money every day for the rest of your life, which is why learning how to become intentional with your money is an imperative skill to acquire. Money is a tool to help you live, enjoy life, and prepare for the future. If you are mindful of how you spend money, impulse spending will no longer be a constant temptation.

Impulse spending is spending money impulsively or based on emotions. It's when you spend money without thinking so that you can fulfill an emotional need that has been unmet.

Table 9.1 Common Reasons People Impulse Spend

Reason	Example
Enjoyment	A person meets a goal at work and decides to celebrate her success by treating herself to a new outfit. This unplanned expense feels acceptable because she works hard and *deserves* this extra purchase.
Status	A man grew up with the best name-brand clothes and items. He now refuses to buy any item that is not from a top brand. The moment he comes across a name brand shirt or outdoor item, he buys it. Owning name-brand items makes him feel important.
Bargain hunting	A person is walking through the store and stops at an aisle endcap marked "75% off." They start picking through the items and easily justify the extra purchase because it's a bargain.
Past money experiences	Someone grew up in a home where their parents spent money without thinking. They saw this firsthand and developed the mindset that it's not important to consider purchases in advance. They continue in their parent's footsteps and spend money without thinking often.
Overcompensating	A parent wants their child to experience a better childhood than they had growing up. They overcompensate for a childhood that felt like it was lacking by spending excessively and impulsively on their own child. The extra spending is easy to justify because it's for their child.
Stress	Someone has a tough day at work. They hate feeling overwhelmed with their workload. To make themselves feel better, they stop by their favorite store on the way home to pick up an item that will lift their spirits.
Boredom	A young woman sits on her sofa at night with her TV on in the background. She's bored and opens the Amazon app on her phone. Without thinking, she starts scrolling and adds items to her cart. She experiences an adrenaline rush and is no longer bored.

Common Reasons People Impulse Spend

Spending money impulsively usually boils down to one thing: emotions. Some people tend to impulse spend when they are stressed, feel like they have no control over their life, or are bored. Spending money is the dopamine hit that helps them avoid the negative emotions they are feeling. However, it's important to remember that it's okay (and—dare I say—healthy) to sit in those emotions at times. We aren't meant to only experience positive emotions. On the contrary, we were created to experience every emotion that life offers.

Table 9.1 outlines several reasons why people tend to spend money impulsively as well as an example of how this could play out in real life.

Can you relate to any of these situations? Maybe you see yourself in one or more of the examples. Learning how to stop impulse spending starts with identifying the patterns in your spending habits.

Find Patterns in Your Past Impulse Spending

It was late at night, and I was the only person awake in my home. Like almost every other night, I was burning the midnight oil and working on building my small business. My plate was full, and I could feel stress settling in my body. I sat at my computer with a to-do list a mile long. That's when I took a deep breath, opened a new tab on my browser, and typed in "amazon.com."

I could feel the tension leave my body as I started searching for new things to buy. Without fail, I added item after item to my cart. I checked out, took a deep breath, and felt *better*.

My stress eased, but I knew deep down that it had only disappeared temporarily. Just a few minutes prior, I felt like I had no control over my workload. Shopping gave me back a sense of control. The only problem? It was a false sense of control.

It took me years to realize that stress and chaos is a major impulse spending trigger for me. But now that I see it, I can't unsee it. These days, when I'm tempted to impulse spend, I remind myself that my desire to spend money is simply a symptom of my stress and it won't fix the real problem.

Am I perfect when it comes to combatting impulse spending? Absolutely not.

Am I making progress when it comes to spending money intentionally? Yes, I am.

Your ability to make progress and grow starts with recognizing and identifying the patterns behind your own impulse spending habits.

When, Where, and Why You Spend Money Impulsively

If you struggle with impulse spending, there are likely patterns when it comes to when, where, and why you spend money spontaneously. It's time to reflect and identify the patterns behind your impulse spending so you can get down to the real reason you're tempted to spend money impulsively.

Start by making a list of the past three to five impulse purchases you've made. Next, take time to analyze the when, where, and why of each purchase.

When: When did you spend money without thinking? What day of the week was it? What time was it?

Where: Where were you when you bought the item(s) impulsively? Was it online or in the store? Were you alone or with others?

Why: What emotions were you feeling *before* you spent money without thinking? What emotions did you have *after* you bought the item(s)?

The point of this exercise is not to make you feel guilty. In fact, in this moment let's decide to be *done* feeling guilty about our past money habits. We did the best we could with what we knew at the time. Now it's time to work on your present and future spending habits.

The goal of this exercise is to reflect on the times when you gave into spending money impulsively so you can put boundaries in place to keep that from happening in the future. Table 9.2 gives an example of how I personally reflected on the *when, where,* and *why* of my late-night Amazon shopping splurge.

Table 9.2   Impulse Spending

Experience	When	Where	Why
Amazon shopping	It was 11:30 p.m. on a weeknight. Everyone else in the house was asleep except me.	I was working on my computer at home alone. I was supposed to be working on writing articles for my business.	Before impulse spending, I felt stressed and overwhelmed. After I spent money, I felt a sense of control.

After thinking through the when, where, and why behind my Amazon shopping splurge, I can easily see that I'm personally tempted to spend impulsively when I'm stressed and alone. It's also a way for me to have a sense of control in my life when I feel like I lack control.

Now it's your turn. Fill out the Impulse Spending Worksheet. Think through five times you've spent money impulsively and dive deep into the when, where, and why of your experience. You can also print the Impulse Spending Worksheet at www.inspiredbudget. com/moneymadeeasy.

Impulse Spending

Experience	When	Where	Why
Describe a time when you spent money impulsively.	*When did you spend money without thinking? What day of the week was it? What time was it?*	*Where were you when you bought the item(s) impulsively? Was it online or in the store? Were you alone or with others?*	*What emotions were you feeling before you spent money without thinking? What emotions did you have after you bought the item(s)?*

Now that you've completed the Impulse Spending Worksheet, it's time to look for patterns in these experiences. When are you tempted to spend money impulsively? Complete the checklist below for everything that is true.

I feel tempted to spend money impulsively when:

☐ It's a certain time of day (example: late at night). If so, what time?

☐ I have been on social media;

☐ Something negative happens in my life;

☐ Something positive happens in my life, and I want to celebrate;

☐ I'm excited or happy;

☐ I'm bored;

- ☐ I see an item on sale;
- ☐ I check my email inbox;
- ☐ I feel sad;
- ☐ I've been home all day;
- ☐ I'm stressed;
- ☐ I've had an argument with someone I love;
- ☐ I want to have control;
- ☐ Other: _____;
- ☐ Other: _____;
- ☐ Other: _____.

Hopefully you have a good understanding of when, where, and maybe even why you have given into impulse spending in the past. Now it's time to get down to the root issue behind your spending.

The Real Reason behind Impulse Spending

Several years ago, we moved into our current home. To say I like our home would be an understatement. Nope, I *love* our home. It sits on a quiet cul-de-sac with a large, tree-filled backyard. The moment I stepped through the door to see this house for the first time, I *knew* it was where I wanted to live.

Once we moved in, my love for this space could not be contained. Determined to make our house everything I dreamed it could be, I filled it with new furniture, art, and ways to keep it organized. Almost every day I shopped online for something new to add to our home.

Within a month, my desire had morphed into an obsession. The excitement and dopamine hit I got after opening another Amazon box was unmatched. Deep down, I knew that my impulse spending had gotten out of hand.

One night after the kids had gone to bed, I sat next to my husband on the sofa. Carefully, he said, "Allison, there's something I want to talk about." I knew instantly where this was headed: my online shopping fixation.

I explained to him that I had started to *crave* online shopping. As crazy as it sounds, I could feel my body gravitating toward it—to the point that I didn't have the willpower to stop myself. We decided that if I was to overcome my impulse spending, I would need clear boundaries around online shopping.

With clear boundaries in place, I was able to free up my mind and determine the *real* reason behind my impulse spending: my desire to provide a comfortable home for our family. A home where my oldest son, who was anxious about starting second grade at a new school, would feel safe. I had guilt about moving him across the state and uprooting him from the only home he knew. To combat these emotions, I did everything in my power to create a home that he, and everyone else, loved. Unfortunately, I tried to do this by falling into the familiar pattern that I had often used to try to make myself happy: shopping. As it turns out, spending money never led to my happiness, and it didn't have anything to do with my son's happiness, either.

As soon as I put my debit card away, I freed up time to work through these emotions. I realized that our house was already a home because we were in it. My son didn't need a perfect house to feel at home. All he needed was me to close the Amazon app, put down my phone, and focus on him.

How to Find the Real Reason

Impulse spending runs deeper than simply not thinking through a purchase before you make it. When you're able to find the true reason behind your money habits, you can treat the real problem.

It took time and reflection for me to pinpoint *why* I was struggling with impulse shopping after moving into our new home. However, once I was able to pinpoint my root issue, my desire to spend money faded.

Review one of the experiences that you included on your Impulse Spending Worksheet. You've listed out the where, when, and why of that experience. Now, answer the following questions about that experience:

1. Did you spend money to *avoid* an emotion?

2. Did you spend money so you could *add* something, or an emotion, to your life?

3. What problem were you trying to fix by spending money?

This work, eye-opening as it is, takes deliberate effort on your part. Don't shy away from this exercise. You might uncover something about yourself that could be life changing.

Battling Comparison

I spent my summers as a child camping along the crystal clear blue water of the Frio River in Texas. My parents would load us up in the car and drive out to the Texas Hill Country, where we would disconnect from the world and our responsibilities for days at a time.

Our afternoons were spent floating down the Frio River, searching for the best rope swings we could find to swing into the cool water. We would roast s'mores at night and stay up past our bedtime by the crackling campfire. My parents even let us bring our bikes, and my brother and I would ride through the campgrounds during the day.

Those moments in my childhood hold a very special place in my heart. Looking back, I realize why they rank as some of my top memories. During those trips, I was living entirely in the moment. I had no care for what others were doing. I wasn't concerned about what I *could* have been doing instead. The thought of comparing my life to someone else's wasn't on my radar.

This, I fully believe, is every child's superpower. Children, especially young children, have the ability to fully live in the moment. They are able to focus solely on what is happening in the present, and everything else disappears. They experience a moment in time fully because at that second, it's all that matters.

Unfortunately, as we grow, a shift takes place. We become more aware of what others are doing, which only highlights what we *are not* doing. By the time I was in my early twenties, I was an expert in comparing my life to others'. It seemed that everyone else was taking trips, had higher salaries, and overall had *more* than me.

The thing about comparison is that when overlooked, it can grow and crystallize in our hearts. The more I compared my life to others, the more I wanted what they had. This led to me spending more money.

Comparison fosters impulse spending. But how do you combat something that you may have been dealing with for years on end? The answer is simple but not necessarily easy. It all comes back to the superpower we once experienced as young children: living in the moment.

How to Live in the Moment

I've been in and out of therapy since I was 14 years old. In the past I would have been embarrassed to share this fact about myself. However, these days I wear my "I have a therapist" badge with honor. One of the things I've been continually working on in therapy is living in the moment.

One day I was sitting across from my therapist, telling her how my fears and worries were keeping me up at night. As soon as my head hit the pillow, my mind would wander, and I'd find myself reliving an uncomfortable situation or worrying about the future. That's when my therapist shared one phrase that changed my life:

Where are your feet planted?

When I worry about a situation that hasn't happened, or one that has already occurred, I ask myself the same question.

Where are your feet planted?

At that moment I think about where I am standing, sitting, or laying. I feel the ground beneath my feet and focus on what is taking place right in front of me. Who is in the room? What am I hearing? What am I doing? I take a minute to intentionally fill my mind with my surroundings, and slowly, my anxieties or worries start to fade away.

Where are your feet planted?

It's a simple question you can ask yourself when you start comparing your house size to someone else's. It's the question to ponder when you see what your friend might be able to afford what you cannot. These five words have helped me learn to live in the moment, just like I was able to do as a young child.

Next time you find yourself comparing your situation, experience, or life to someone else's I want you to stop, refocus your mind, and think about where your feet are planted. Bring yourself back to the moment happening in time. It's in this moment that you can learn to become content with the life you are living.

Social Media and Advertising

One "lightbulb moment" in my life was when I realized the impact that social media had on my tendency to spend money impulsively.

It can be easy to ignore commercials or sponsored posts that are clearly targeting you to purchase a product.

However, I've found that I, and others, struggle more with impulse spending when it comes to seeing what friends and family share on social media. There have been times when I was scrolling through social media, and I see a friend's post. I immediately want what they have. And guess what—that thing they have usually costs money.

Have you been in this situation before?

Have you ever found yourself scrolling through your social media only to see that someone bought the latest phone, went on a nice vacation, or splurged on a new robot vacuum cleaner that cleans their floor while they sit back and watch TV?

That's when it hits you: You want what they have. Next thing you know, you are scrolling Amazon for the latest vacuum cleaner that might cost you a full day's paycheck. Ultimately, you are reacting emotionally to what you are seeing on social media, whether that's a store advertisement or an old high school friend's latest post.

The key to overcoming comparison on social media is to challenge your thinking. This looks like deliberately changing your thoughts from what they are to something that will serve you better. Table 9.3: Challenge Your Thinking gives examples of how you can do this when scrolling on social media.

As you're scrolling social media, become aware of what you are consuming. Remember that what people post on social media is not a reflection of what you have or don't have.

Table 9.3 Challenge Your Thinking

Instead of:	Try This:
"I need that item."	"They are selling an item that I don't need."
"I want that item."	"I'm happy with the things I have."
"Why can't I take a vacation too?"	"Their family is making memories. I can make memories anywhere."

Responding to Impulse Spending in the Moment

It's been over 10 years since starting my journey of working on my money mindset, and I still struggle with impulse spending. I've made progress, but I'm not perfect. There are still times that I am tempted to spend money impulsively. And yes, there are times that I follow through on those impulses.

However, I have learned how to minimize impulse spending by responding to these desires in the moment. This is exactly what you can do as well. Here are three things you can do the next time you find yourself in a situation where you're tempted to spend money spontaneously.

1. Question Your Thoughts

To stop impulse spending in its tracks, you must learn how to question the thoughts that enter your mind. We already discussed in Chapter 2, "Money Habits and Money Mindset," that your thoughts can lie to you. Thankfully, you are in control of your thinking.

Below are five questions to ask yourself when a scarcity money thought or money lie enters your mind:

1. Is this money thought true?

2. How do you feel or react when you believe this money thought?

3. How do you treat yourself when you believe this thought?

4. What if you didn't have this money thought? How would you feel? Would it have an impact on your confidence to handle money?

5. How can you replace this thought with one that serves you better?

You can ask these same questions when you're tempted to spend money impulsively. Let's look at an example.

You've been working all day, and you're on your way home. Even though you have food that you can cook at home, the thought "I'm too tired to cook. Maybe I should pick up dinner instead" enters your mind.

At that moment, you pause and ask yourself, "Is this thought true? Am I so tired that I cannot cook a quick and easy meal?" Chances are you do have enough energy to throw together a fast meal. You then replace the thought with "I have enough energy to make a quick dinner at home."

By simply asking yourself one question, you're able to refocus on the money boundaries you've set for yourself.

2. Sit with Your Feelings

Every spring my allergies are triggered by the oak pollen that falls from the mature trees in our area. And every spring, I am miserable. I cannot stop sneezing, my nose is stopped up, and I dread walking outside. This past spring, I was laying in my bed with a box of tissues and started googling ways to help my allergies aside from my trusty Claritin-D.

That's when I stumbled upon an article about an air purifier. I spent several minutes reading about one air purifier that cleans 99% of the air. One of the benefits, you guessed it, is fewer allergic reactions.

I clicked the link, and it led me straight to Amazon. The air purifier I had been eyeing cost a whopping $350! I read the reviews (which were raving, by the way) and considered the cost. In that moment, I was tempted to buy it with one click. I was tired of feeling sick, and *this was the answer to my problem.*

That's when I paused. I allowed myself to be frustrated in that moment. I allowed myself to temporarily hate the beautiful oak trees that made this happen. I decided that instead of buying the air purifier right away, I would find a way to include it in our next budget. Simply sitting with my feelings for a few minutes allowed me to clear my mind and come up with a plan for how I could buy the air purifier without overspending.

We've already established that your thoughts can lie to you. Too often these thoughts lead to uncomfortable feelings. Most of the time they are feelings that challenge us and can even lead to impulse spending.

Here's the truth: Feelings aren't bad. It's perfectly natural to have feelings of sadness and jealousy. The issue is that too often we allow these feelings to dictate our spending habits. It's time to learn to sit with your feelings, even if it's uncomfortable. Instead of immediately buying an item to help you feel better, try sitting with those feelings. Let them sink in. Then, come up with a plan for what you will do next.

3. Take Action

Once you've questioned your thoughts and have taken the time to sit with your feelings, you're ready to take action. This is when you'll decide what you will do or what boundaries you will set surrounding the purchase that you want to make. This can be as simple as deciding you're not going to buy the item to adding it to your budget like I did with the air purifier.

Below are some examples of how you can take action in the moment.

- Add the item you want to buy to a wish list;
- Set up a sinking fund for the item;

- Add it to your budget;

- Decide to not buy the item;

- Think it over for a week.

Conquering impulse spending won't happen overnight. It's a skill that develops over time with practice and intention. Have compassion and grace for yourself as you work through this process.

What to Do after You've Spent Impulsively

So you've spent money impulsively. *Now what?*

As you work on your money habits, it's important to remember that perfection is a myth. It doesn't exist, so don't expect perfection for yourself. There will be moments when you'll be tempted to impulse spend. There will even be times that you follow through with the temptation of spending money impulsively. Instead of becoming angry with yourself and giving up on conquering impulse spending altogether, learn to have compassion for yourself and face your consequences.

The next time you spend money impulsively, answer the following questions to help you think through how you can prevent this from happening in the future.

1. What did you buy?

2. What were you feeling before you bought the item?

3. Did you try to resist the impulse purchase?

4. How did you feel after you bought the item?

5. Are you going to keep the item or return it?

6. How do you need to adjust your budget now?

While we can't expect perfection, we can expect *reflection*. When you've gone overboard with spending money, reflect on the real reason behind your spending. Get down to the root issue so you can create boundaries in your life that will help you be successful with your money.

Tips to Help with Impulse Spending

The answer to eliminating impulse spending from your life comes down to identifying the bigger reason behind your temptation to spend money. However, it's also nice to have a few tips you can follow and implement every day to reduce the temptation a little more. Here are my top 12 tips to help with impulse spending.

1. Include Spending Money in Your Budget

Including spending money, or pocket money, in your budget while working to pay off debt or save money might sound counterintuitive, but it's not. When you set aside money to spend on whatever you want, you are creating a clear boundary for your money. This allows you to spend money guilt-free while still working to meet your financial goals.

Ultimately, allowing room in your budget for spending takes your original budget and turns it into a realistic budget. It gives you room to still feel like you can spend money on what you want, while being successful with money. This builds up your financial confidence and can even help you avoid impulse spending.

2. Unsubscribe from Store Emails

If you're trying to stop spending money impulsively, then the last thing you need popping up in your inbox each day is an email listing out all the deals and offers that your favorite store is offering. Hit the unsubscribe button. You won't regret it.

3. Unfollow or Mute Temptations on Social Media

Your favorite retail stores have entire teams that work on their social media accounts. Their sole job is to create content that is designed to make you want to buy something or head to their store. If you've noticed that your favorite stores on social media are triggers for you, then remove them from your feed. You have complete control over what you see on social media, so stop allowing content that tempts you to overspend.

4. Keep Your Debit Card at Home

You're walking through the store for just a few things. That's when something catches your eye, so you toss it in your cart. "What's an extra $9?" you think. But when that happens five or six times, it adds up quick. To help break this habit, don't bring your debit card with you in the store. Instead, count out exactly how much money you'll need in cash to buy those items, and only bring that. You'll be forced to stick to your list.

5. Use Cash Envelopes

If it wasn't for cash envelopes, our family would likely spend an extra $300 each month on restaurants than we normally do. Each paycheck we decide how much money we want to budget for going out to eat. We pull that amount out in cash and place it in an envelope. This allows us to easily see how much money we have spent, and how much money we have left to spend on restaurants. It creates a boundary and stopping point for our spending.

Whether you spend impulsively on food, home décor items, or clothes, cash envelopes can help. Try using cash envelopes for one category in your budget where you have found that you are tempted to overspend.

6. Let Items Sit in Your Cart

If you struggle with online shopping, this tip is for you. The next time you come across something online that you want to buy, let the item sit in your cart for a few days. If you still want it in a week, then find a way to save up for the item or add it to your next budget.

You might be surprised that sometimes the desire to buy the item fades. Allowing an item to sit in your cart for a week gives you time and space to determine whether it's something you actually want to spend money on.

7. Find an Accountability Partner

Saying no to impulse spending can be hard when you're just getting started. To help you stay on track, ask a friend or partner to be your accountability partner. Talk to them about your spending goals, and let them hold you accountable when you want to impulse buy. Ask them for a pep talk or words of encouragement. Even just checking in with someone can have a big impact on your temptation to spend money impulsively.

8. Calculate the Cost in Hours Worked

Sometimes all it takes to deter me from buying an expensive product is to think of how many hours I'll have to work to pay for that product. For example, let's say you make $25 an hour. You're browsing through your favorite store and before you know it you're about to spend $350 on items that you didn't intend to buy. Take a moment to do the math. It will take you fourteen hours of work to pay for those items. Thinking about your spending this way might keep you from checking out altogether.

9. Remove Your Card Information Online

Stores have made it incredibly easy to spend money online these days. They've made impulse shopping second nature. Many online stores give you the option of storing your debit or credit card info online. This makes it even easier for you to buy an item with just one click. The extra step of manually entering your payment information gives you another minute to think through your purchase before you make the final decision.

10. Stay out of the Stores

There was a time in my life that I had zero self-control when I walked into any Target store. I'd head in for two items and walk out forty-five minutes later with my intended items *plus* a new tank top, cute picture frame, and fake plant. I knew deep down that I had to stop letting Target take all my money. I decided to start limiting how often I would go inside the store. I called it my "Target Detox." I needed time and space to separate myself from the store.

The less often you walk into a store or open your Internet browser to shop, the less often you'll be tempted to spend money impulsively. While you don't have to eliminate stores altogether, you can focus on limiting how often you shop. A good way to start is by only making one grocery run each week if possible. Stopping by the grocery store a few times each week gives you another opportunity to impulse spend.

11. Find Something Free or Low Cost

Sometimes I'm tempted to spend money because I'm bored. Buying an item that I want makes me feel better and fills my time. One way to overcome money spending habits is to replace them with rewarding activities that are free or low cost. My favorites include taking my dog on a walk, listening to podcasts that tell a story, and playing basketball outside with my two sons. Check out the list below for even more low-cost or free activities you can try out.

- Go on a bike ride;
- Go to the library;
- Visit a museum;
- Play a board game;
- Call a friend;
- Organize a space in your home;
- Go on a hike;
- Cook a new recipe;
- Volunteer;
- Get crafty and make something;
- Learn a new skill;
- Exercise.

Get creative and have fun when you're searching for a free or low-cost activity to replace your desire to impulse spend.

12. Focus on What You Want Long Term

There's no other way around it: impulse shopping and overspending will delay your ability to reach your money goals. One way to combat impulse spending is to remind yourself about what you truly want long term in your life when it comes to your money. Do you want to be able to travel the world without going into debt? Or maybe you want to help support your children as they head to college or get their first job in the real world. Focusing on your bigger goals when you're tempted to spend money impulsively might be just what you need to stay on track with your money.

Replacing Impulse with Intention

While you can't expect perfection when it comes to your spending habits, you can recognize and celebrate the progress that you make as you work to change your relationship with money. As you focus your awareness and intention, you build your ability to control your impulses. It might take time, but conquering impulse spending will be worth all your effort.

Action Items

- Complete the Impulse Spending Worksheet to find patterns in your spending habits.
- Think about one time you've spent money in the past. Answer the following questions about that experience:
  - Did you spend money to avoid an emotion?
  - Did you spend money so you could add something or an emotion to your life?
  - What problem were you trying to fix by spending money?
- When you're tempted to impulse spend, question your thoughts in the moment, sit with your feelings, and take action.
- Choose three tips you will implement in your life to help with impulse spending. Circle the three that you will start doing.

- Include spending money in your budget;
- Unsubscribe from store emails;
- Keep your debit card at home;
- Use cash envelopes;
- Let items sit in your cart;
- Find an accountability partner;
- Calculate the cost in hours worked;
- Remove your card information online;
- Stay out of the stores;
- Find something free or low-cost.
- Focus on what you want long term.

Chapter 10

Working with Your Partner

Sometimes people experience seasons in their lives where they find themselves incredibly busy. Matt and I are no different. Between working full time, raising two children, and trying to keep up with life's daily demands, sometimes there isn't a lot of time left in the day to communicate.

One January, when we found ourselves in a very busy season, Matt approached me with an idea. He suggested that every Sunday night we have a meeting. He called it our "Family business meeting." He thought that if we held weekly family business meetings, we could dedicate time to communicate about the "business" parts of our lives for the upcoming week. I figured we had nothing to lose, so we blocked off 30 minutes every Sunday on our shared family calendar.

During this time together, we got on the same page about everything going on in our lives. We discussed the upcoming week's work schedules, after-school activities for the kids, our meal plan for the week, and we even looked over our budget and spending.

The purpose behind these weekly family business meetings was simple: dedicate 30 minutes to discuss these topics and spend the rest of our week enjoying a conversation about *anything* else. These simple yet powerful weekly meetings transformed the way we communicated and allowed us to get on the same page about work schedules, money, and even our goals. It was a true turning point for us in terms of communicating and working *together*.

Learning how to effectively communicate properly and manage your finances as a couple can be a daunting task. However, with the right strategies in place, like weekly family business meetings, it might be easier than you imagined.

Communication Is Key

Communicating with your spouse about all areas of your life is important, but communicating about money is vital to the success of your marriage and your future. Think about it this way: money seeps into your life every single day. Each day you make choices that tie back to your finances. Choices such as:

- Whether or not to book a vacation on your credit card;
- Whether there's room in your budget to grab takeout instead of cooking at home;
- Whether you can afford to outsource household chores such as cleaning and lawn maintenance;
- How to make sure you have enough money to cover your monthly expenses; and
- Which stores you can, and cannot, afford to shop at.

These small and seemingly simple choices all tie back to money. When money is stressful, these minor decisions can become quite overwhelming. Getting on the same page financially with your spouse has hundreds of benefits. While I could fill this entire book with them, I'll leave you with a few that I believe are most important.

Benefits of positive communication surrounding money:

- You no longer feel like you're working on your money alone, and instead you're working as a team;

- You have a built-in accountability partner to help you stay on track and reach your goals;

- If you have children, you are giving them the opportunity to learn what communication about money looks like in real life;

- When you work together, you are more likely to reach your money goals;

- Your communication in other areas of your life improves as well;

- You learn to be a more compassionate person who extends grace to others.

Communicating with your spouse about money is so much more than just talking about money. It's laying a solid foundation of teamwork and grace for your relationship, your family, and generations to come.

How to Discuss Budgeting and Money with Your Partner

Matt and I never discussed money while we were dating or engaged. By the time we were married, we realized we were long overdue for an honest and open conversation about our finances. As you can imagine, when money is stressful, conversations can be tense as well. I'm not going to lie—we experienced many arguments and tears as we worked through the best way to communicate about money.

If you and your partner have never discussed money or finances in the past, you might be unsure about how to start the conversation in a way that allows you to both feel heard and respected. Throw in any past financial trauma or money stress, and you might be walking on eggshells around your partner when money comes up in conversation.

No matter your past, it's worth the effort to get on the same page with your partner. The benefits far outweigh any difficult conversations that you may have. In fact, these moments may even provide you with an opportunity to grow closer to your partner. Ready to get started? The next four tips offer a solution for creating an open and honest space to communicate about money in your relationship.

1. Discuss Your Dreams and Goals

You might be tempted to sit down with your partner and jump right into the math behind your finances. It's natural to want to immediately discuss your expenses, where you're overspending, and how much debt you have. This is great in theory, but I'd like you to try this instead: the next time you discuss money with your partner, start by having a conversation about your dreams and goals for your future.

What would you do if you didn't have anything holding you back? If you didn't have debt payments standing in your way, how would you spend any leftover money? Maybe you'd donate to a charity you would be proud to support. Or maybe you'd fulfill your dream of transitioning to part-time work instead of a full-time job. The options for your dreams are endless.

A shift takes place when you're willing to speak your dreams out loud. Something that never felt possible suddenly feels more *real*. Take time to write out your family's dreams and goals on paper and post it somewhere in your home. Come back to these goals as you work on the math of your money. The decisions you make surrounding your money should take you one step closer to your shared goal.

2. Focus on the Benefits

We all know that there are pros and cons to almost everything we do in life. The same goes for taking the time to plan out where your money will go each month. I tend to be a glass-half-full person in general, but six years ago, when we started budgeting, I had to train myself to stay positive when it came to budgeting as a team.

When you're planning how to spend your money for the upcoming pay period, it's easy to focus on what you're not getting in the moment. Whining and complaining come naturally. It's much harder to delay gratification and live on less than you make. The good news is that you can do hard things. Start by thinking through what doors budgeting alongside your partner can open for you.

What is it that you and your partner hope to gain by living on a budget? Are you two hoping to reach financial freedom from debt? What about the ability to buy a big-ticket item such as a new car? Or maybe it's a down payment on your dream home?

Whatever it is, remind yourself and your partner to focus on the benefits of budgeting, even when it's difficult. Focus on what you are building together for the future, not on what you may be missing out on in the present. The goal here is to change your mindset when it comes to managing your money.

3. Provide Concrete Examples

If your partner is hesitant to budget, come to the conversation prepared with concrete examples of what budgeting would look like for your family. Before you meet with your partner, draft a sample budget, and bring it with you to discuss the idea of living on a budget. Sometimes people dismiss an idea because they cannot envision all the benefits that it might bring to their life.

Instead of saying, "I think we need to get on a budget. We spend way too much money on (insert item here)," try approaching your spouse with the problem *and* a possible solution. The solution is the sample budget you created. This is perfect for anyone who is a visual learner and needs to *see* a plan in action.

4. Allow Room for Fun

Just because you are on a budget doesn't mean you can't have fun or spend money on what you want. Next time you write a budget, include spending money for each person. This spending money can be used for anything you or your partner wants. Each person can have their own separate amount, or you can combine it together into one amount.

When you both have a set amount of money to spend on something fun, you'll be more willing to sit down and work together on the budget each month. Plus, you'll be much more likely to stick to your budget in the long run.

Approaching a Reluctant Partner

You might be reading this book alongside a partner who is on board with learning how to write a budget that will benefit your family. Both of you are on the same page and want to communicate better about money. If that's the case, I want you to pause and go give your partner a high five right now!

However, maybe you're reading this book all by yourself. Your partner is not on board with the idea of budgeting, and to be honest, you might even be thinking there's absolutely no way you can get them on the same page with you about money.

No matter where you or your partner stand when it comes to being on the same page about money, I want you to have hope. Many people are reluctant to talk about money due to their own money trauma, which we discussed in Chapter 2, "Money Habits and Money Mindset." If your partner grew up in a family where their parents or guardians fought about money, divorced over money, or never discussed money, then they might have trauma around finances. Childhood trauma can take root deep into our hearts without us even realizing it's there.

So what's the best way to approach a partner who is reluctant to discuss money?

The simple answer: Patiently.

The complicated answer: Patiently. Your partner might not be open to discussing money right away. You might have to plant the seed weeks or even months in advance. It could take time for them to adjust their own money mindset to see that managing money together is important and beneficial to your relationship. While I would love to guarantee you that you won't have to do this alone, here's the truth: *there might be times when you feel alone.* But just because your partner isn't sitting next to you writing a budget and creating money goals doesn't mean they won't be there one day.

Four Tips for Approaching a Reluctant Partner

Determined to get your partner on the same page with you when it comes to your money? If so, start with the four tips below.

1. Know Your Spouse and When to Approach Them

My husband *loves* football. When we started dating, I didn't fully realize the extent of his love for the sport, which I couldn't care less about. There were many times in our relationship when a football game was on TV, and I would start talking to Matt about our plans for the week. He always responded in one of two ways: silence or he would say, "Sure."

I bet you know where this is headed. Later in the week I'd talk about the plans we had made, and he had *zero* recollection of our conversation. At the beginning of our relationship, it even led to a few arguments. I learned through trial and error to have important conversations with Matt before or after a football game.

◆

He had to learn the same about me. If I'm listening to a podcast or reading a book, I will zone out to any conversation that's happening around me. I might even respond to him with a "yes" or "no," and minutes later have no memory of what I agreed to.

There's a time and place for important conversations. Over the years Matt and I had to learn when we should and shouldn't approach the other person about money.

You know your partner better than anyone. Take a moment to think about *when* the best time is to discuss your finances. Is it right after dinner or maybe after they've had their morning coffee? The goal is to approach your partner when they can focus their attention on you and are open to having this type of conversation.

2. Come with a Solution in Mind

When you're stressed about money, it's easy to focus on your financial frustrations. While it's perfectly okay to have these feelings, laying them all on a reluctant partner can easily overwhelm them. Before you approach your partner about getting on board with money, start by brainstorming possible solutions for your financial problem.

For example, if you find yourself living paycheck to paycheck, then possible solutions include writing a budget, paying off debt to reduce monthly payments, and tracking your spending. Even setting up a sinking fund for upcoming expenses such as back-to-school clothes or braces for the kids can be seen as a solution.

By coming to the table with possible solutions (they don't have to be perfect by any means), your partner might be more likely to listen because you aren't spending the entire time focusing on just the problem.

3. Use a Kind and Respectful Tone

I don't know about your partner, but when I approach my husband with a disrespectful or unkind tone, a wall goes up. He doesn't want to be talked to this way, and I honestly can't blame him. Money is emotional. When your finances become stressful, those emotions can easily present themselves as anger and frustration. This is a completely normal response. However, it's important to remember that while you may be angry or frustrated, you can still start the conversation in a respectful way. And this is a two-way street, too. If your partner is expressing themselves in a frustrated way that starts to go too far, ask them to try to be more respectful and considerate of you.

Starting off a conversation in a positive tone is more likely to get you farther than if you come into the conversation yelling. Give it a try, and see whether the results are different.

4. Let Them See the Change

One woman that I worked with in the past had a partner who wasn't on board with budgeting. She was ready to get their money organized and develop a plan to help them pay off debt and start investing. What ultimately helped him get on board was allowing him to see the change that she was making.

First, she wrote all her bills on a calendar and hung the calendar on the fridge. As she paid each bill, she crossed it off. Because the calendar was hanging in a common space, he saw it every single day. Eventually he started asking questions. He saw the progress that she was making and witnessed this one small change that she had made. As it turns out, he wanted to learn more about what she was doing.

By allowing him to see the change in the way she interacted with their money, he became eager to get on board.

What's one small change that you want to make with your money? Do you want to pay off debt? If so, create a debt payoff plan and hang it in a common space. Cross off the debts as you pay them or color in a visual as you make progress. As your partner sees the change taking place, they will realize that not only is it important to you, but these changes come with amazing benefits.

Weekly Money Meetings

One of the best things you can do to improve your relationship and finances is to start scheduling weekly budget meetings. Hate the sound of the word "meeting"? Then call it a budget date. Whatever you do, this type of weekly meeting with your partner will be extremely beneficial when you want to get on the same page with your money.

A budget meeting is just what it sounds like. It's a meeting you and your partner set to discuss your budget, money, or any other family business.

If your partner isn't on board, then start having these meetings by yourself. No one ever said you need someone else to make it an official meeting. Who knows—maybe your significant other will pick up on what you're doing and want to join you.

Don't Underestimate Your Budget Meeting

Budget meetings act as a check-in when it comes to the important areas of your life. Have you ever noticed that it's easy to become sidetracked when it comes to your money goals? Maybe you know you need to be budgeting, but after two weeks you've thrown in the towel and assume budgets just won't work for your family.

Budget meetings offer you a weekly check-in so you don't give up on your journey. They act as touch points so that you can get yourself back on track and keep working toward your money goals. Even more importantly, budget meetings are a way for you and your partner to get (and stay!) on the same page about money.

Make Budget Meetings Nonnegotiable

I'd like to say that my husband and I *never* miss our weekly family budget meeting, but that would be a lie. I can tell you though, when we do miss a meeting, we lose sight of our goals for the week. When you're just getting started on this money journey, make these meetings nonnegotiable.

Think of it this way: if you have a cavity or toothache, you wouldn't put off going to the dentist, especially if it's incredibly painful. Nope, you would make sure to schedule a dentist appointment, and you wouldn't miss it for the world.

You can think about your budget meeting the same way. These intentional times together will be vital to the growth of your finances and relationship. Here are a few tips to help you make sure you don't miss a budget meeting (especially in the beginning):

- Have the meeting on the same day and time every single week.
- Add the meeting to your calendar as well as your partner's calendar.
- If you have children, make sure they know you'll be having an important meeting every week. They are welcome to attend (if it's okay with you) or tell them you shouldn't be interrupted during your budget meeting. Setting clear boundaries for children will minimize distractions during this time.
- Choose a day and time that is easy and works for both of you. For instance, Matt and I have our budget meetings on Sunday

nights after dinner. We rarely have activities during this time, and we are usually at home together. This day and time for our family makes sense. Find a time that makes sense for your family.

Choose a day and time to have your weekly budget meetings, and record that day and time below. Then, go add it to your phone or personal calendar.

Our weekly budget meeting will be on _____ at _____.

Budget Meeting Expectations

Before you sit down for your first budget meeting, spend 10 minutes setting clear expectations for what is and is not allowed. When money is stressful in a relationship, tensions can run high, which can lead people to say something that harms your financial progress as a couple.

To keep that from happening and to keep you *wanting* to continue these weekly budget meetings, it's important to set expectations and rules.

Table 10.1 provides a list of Do's and Don'ts for our personal budget meetings. Feel free to use the same list of expectations for your meetings as well:

Table 10.1 Personal Budget Meeting Expectations

Do	Don't
• Come with an open mind	• Come with an attitude or use an unkind tone
• Work as a team	
• Respect any boundaries	• Point fingers and blame your partner
• Give grace	• Bombard your partner when they least expect it
• Use a kind tone	
• Have a plan for what you will discuss	• Focus on the past
• Take a break if you need one	• Give up on your goal
• Make it fun	

Budget meetings can be extremely beneficial. To get the most out of them, commit to them weekly. As you learn how to communicate effectively with your partner about money, these meetings will get easier and who knows, you might even look forward to them each week.

What to Discuss

Have you ever walked into a work meeting and had no clue what was on the agenda? You're left wondering if you should have prepared something in advance or if this meeting is entirely pointless. Well, we don't want your weekly budget meetings to be like that.

Below is a list of what you and your partner can discuss during your weekly budget meetings. Pick and choose what you would like to discuss. Just remember that you can talk about *anything* during these meetings. While it's important to discuss your budget and money goals, feel free to also discuss any family commitments as well.

Below is a list of topics and action items for your weekly budget meetings. Pick and choose what works for you:

- Write a new budget;
- Follow up on your current budget:
  - Is it working?
  - If not, what can you do to reset the budget?
- Update spending tracker;
- Update debt tracker;
- Set new monthly goals;
- Update monthly goals:
  - Are you on track to meet your monthly goal?
  - What do you need to do differently to meet your monthly goal?

- Pay bills if necessary;
- Discuss this week's meal plan:
  - What are you eating each night?
  - Who is cooking which meals?
- Discuss this week's evening activities;
- Set three small weekly goals (example: cook dinner at home six nights, eat together as a family five nights, and exercise four times);
- Discuss any upcoming large expenses:
  - What do you need to start saving for now?
- Other: _____;
- Other: _____.

You're ready to have your first budget meeting! Remember to make these fun. Open a bottle of wine or make a delicious snack for these meetings. Just because you're discussing money doesn't mean this time together has to be boring.

Joint vs. Separate Bank Accounts

You might be wondering if you and your partner should have joint or separate bank accounts. While I believe that either option is fine, I think it depends on what works best for you and your partner. Let's look at the benefits of joint accounts, separate accounts, and a mix of both.

Benefits of Joint Bank Accounts

A joint bank account is the same as any normal account, yet both you and your partner have equal access to the money. This typically means that you each have your own debit card that can pull money from this account.

Some of the benefits of joint accounts include:

- Full transparency with knowing how money is being spent;
- You each have a clear overall financial picture;
- Joint accounts encourage teamwork when it comes to working on the money;
- Can make budgeting easier and more streamlined.

Joint accounts are great for those who are newly married or want to work on their finances hand in hand.

Benefits of Separate Bank Accounts

While joint bank accounts work for some, they aren't for everyone. People choose not to blend their money for many reasons. These reasons can be very personal and should be respected by the other person. Sometimes a partner comes into a marriage with negative money experiences from a past relationship or childhood. Others might get married later in life and would rather keep their finances separate.

Separate bank accounts offer great benefits for couples:

- Each person has more autonomy or control of their money;
- Eliminates two people withdrawing money at the same time;
- Provides bank account diversification in case of fraud.

I've known many marriages that are successful, and both partners have kept their finances entirely separate. No matter how you choose to keep your money organized, know that this does not dictate the success of your marriage.

Joint and Separate Bank Accounts

A wonderful compromise to the banking question is to have both joint and separate accounts. This is perfect for couples who want to share the costs of bills but also want their own account for spending money.

Here's how this works:

1. Income is deposited into a joint checking account. This is the same account that all the household bills are paid from.

2. Each couple transfers money out of the joint checking account into a separate personal account. This is where each person can keep their own spending money.

3. Rinse and repeat!

Another option is to have your income automatically deposited into separate accounts. Then, each person can transfer money into a joint account to cover bills and necessary expenses.

Essentially, each person in the relationship has their own autonomy and can make spending decisions on their own. This is a great solution for people who want to work together to pay bills but still keep their money separated.

Compromise Is Everything

When a couple takes the first step to getting on the same page about money there will likely be a few missteps and miscommunication along the way. You both might not agree on every single decision, and that's okay. You are human, after all.

Many times, marriage comes down to compromise.

Compromise on where to go out to eat for dinner.
Compromise on what TV show to watch after the kids go to bed.
Compromise on how to spend your money.

There's no other way around it. If you are married, you will have to compromise when it comes to your finances. You can't always have it your way, and neither can your partner. While that can be frustrating at times, compromise means you are both getting a say in what you do with the household money.

Compromise looks like this:

- Your family receives a large tax refund. One person wants to send the entire refund to debt. The other person wants to use the refund to pay for a summer vacation. A good compromise would be to send half to debt and use the other half for a budget-friendly vacation.

- While writing the budget, the "spender" in the relationship has a $100 spending limit each month while the saver has a $75 spending limit. This is what our family did for years. I had more spending money than my husband for several reasons. While this might not appear fair to anyone outside our family, it worked as a wonderful compromise so that we could reach our money goals.

- One person wants to spend $500 on a new gadget while the other person would rather save the money. A good compromise would be saving $100 each month until you can afford the purchase with cash.

Overall, it's important to remember that your goal is to work together and be on the same page. I'm guessing you both want the same thing: to help your family live a financially free life. But to get to where you want to be, there will be big (and small) decisions that will require compromise along the way.

I have no doubt that you and your partner can get on the same page about money. I believe that together you can reach your money goals—no matter how far-fetched they may feel at this moment. But to get to where you want to be, you must start.

Action Items

- Choose a day and time for your weekly budget meetings;
- Create your own list of expectations for your budget meetings;
- Choose what you will discuss during your budget meetings;
- Decide how you will organize your finances with your partner:
  - Joint checking account;
  - Separate checking accounts;
  - Both.

Chapter 11

Accelerating Your Financial Progress

When I was in college, my degree plan included four full years of classes followed by a semester-long student teaching experience. While most of my classmates took the entire four and a half years to complete their degree, I was determined to finish in four years and step out into the real world six months early.

To reach my goal, I loaded up my schedule when it came to taking classes. Not only did I take a full load of classes during the regular semesters, but I also took classes over the summer at a community college. I was willing to do whatever it took to speed up the college process.

Sometimes we are driven enough that we are willing to make sacrifices in the present to reach our goal sooner. That was me. I was eager to push through my college experience while other people I knew traveled in the summer and took a lighter course load throughout the year.

I had the same enthusiasm when my husband, Matt, and I were working to pay off debt. Our original timeline was to become debt free in five years. This felt like an *eternity* at the time, but I figured we could accelerate our debt-free journey, even if it was by just a few months. While we didn't live on Ramen noodles or skip out on date nights entirely, we did make thoughtful decisions and sacrifices along the way to reach our goal sooner.

If you're willing to sacrifice for a *season*, you can live the rest of your life in *abundance*.

You might feel the same way. Maybe you have debt hanging over your head, and you're ready to do whatever it takes to get it gone as soon as possible. Or maybe you've realized that you want to retire a few years earlier than you planned, so you're ready to speed up your retirement savings.

No matter whether you want to accelerate a short-term goal or a long-term goal, every dollar counts. Let's talk about ways that you can make faster progress with your money goals.

Follow the Plan You Set

Your budget is simply a plan for your money. Following your plan for your money will allow you to take another step closer to your goals. Now, I'll be the first to admit that following a budget isn't always easy, especially when you enjoy spending money like I do. However, when I'm able to focus on writing a realistic budget or creating a plan that is doable, I'm more likely to follow through on it.

While working to pay off debt, Matt and I would write a budget that allowed us to send extra money to debt. We were sending more money to debt than I thought was possible because we had every penny accounted for in our budget.

If you want to speed up the process when it comes to reaching your money goals, the *very* first step is to write a budget and follow it. This is your secret weapon when it comes to reaching your money goals. It's the thing that separates the people who reach their money goals from those who don't. It all comes down to being intentional with your budget each pay period.

The same is true for *any* money goal you have. If you want to pay off your child's braces faster, intentionally send extra money to that expense in your budget. If you want to retire sooner, intentionally allocate more of your paycheck for your 401(k). Yes, your net pay will be less each month, but if you write a budget and live on less, you can enjoy a higher nest egg later in life.

Decrease Expenses and Spending

While Matt and I were working to pay off debt, we were notified by our employer that our health insurance costs would be increasing by $150 each month. This meant that our salary would remain the same, but we would be bringing home less money due to rising health insurance costs.

We were faced with a decision. If we wanted to continue paying off the same amount of debt each month, we would have to find $150 to cut from our budget and spending. We immediately sat down to look over our expenses and spending. We combed through our bank statements and had tough conversations about what we were willing to remove permanently from our spending and what we were willing to spend less on.

Ultimately, we landed on shopping around for a less expensive car insurance plan, which would save us money each month as well as canceling cable. Now, let me be clear with you. We canceled cable before it was cool. This was before you could stream Netflix and Hulu to your TV. Instead of paying $75 each month for cable, we installed an obnoxious antenna on our roof that allowed us to have access to basic channels.

When making this decision, we had to ask ourselves what our priority was. For us, it was to continue our debt-free journey at the same speed. Do you want to know the best part of this decision? Instead of having the TV on all the time in the background, we started playing music in our home. Our kids grew to love music, and it encouraged us to turn off distractions and dance to the music filling our home.

On the outside looking in, we appeared to lose our access to cable entertainment. But on the inside, we eliminated a major distraction while filling our home with music. And of course, we continued to pay off debt during the process.

If you want to pay off debt faster, save more money, or prioritize investing, then it's time to look through your expenses and spending. Ask yourself what you're willing to reduce, or even remove, from your life and spending. You don't have to reduce or remove this *forever*. It could mean cutting back for just a season. This practice also encourages you to spend based on your values. It's just one piece of the puzzle when it comes to speeding up your debt-free journey.

Complete an Expense Audit

Any time I want to reduce my spending so I can reach a money goal faster, I always complete an audit on the four largest categories of my spending: housing, food, transportation, and insurance. I figure that if I can reduce my spending in the four categories below, it will free up more cash flow each month *and* allow me to make a Starbucks run every Friday.

The four budget categories below have a major impact on your spending. I've included ideas on how to reduce your spending in each of these areas.

Housing

- If you own your home, can you refinance to a lower interest rate to save money both monthly and in the long run?
- If you rent, can you negotiate your rent price or even move to a more affordable rental?
- Is there a way to reduce your landscaping costs overall?

Food

- Can you reduce your grocery budget by 5–10% each month?

- Are you buying more food at the grocery store than you need? Meal planning helps ensure that you're only buying the food you need.

- Can you reduce your restaurant budget by 10% each month? You can still enjoy dinner out while finding extra money in your budget.

Transportation

- If your car payment is out of control, can you try trading in your car for a less expensive car? This could help lower your monthly payments significantly.

- Can you refinance your car loan for a lower interest rate? Check out local credit unions in your area for lower rates.

- Can you save money on gas by carpooling or riding a bike to different locations? This might not be feasible for everyone, but it could help you save money overall.

Insurance

- Spending just 30 minutes once a year shopping around for more affordable car insurance and home insurance can save you serious money. This is one of the tasks that you do once and enjoy the savings all year long.

- Are you overpaying for life insurance? Consider switching to term life insurance. It's more affordable and still gives you great coverage.

By taking a few hours to look over your expenses, you'll be able to find ways to spend less *all year long*. Each of these expenses can add up exponentially over time.

Increase Your Income

While Matt and I were on our debt-free journey, we were working together at a small school district in Texas. One year, he decided to take a new job as a band director in a different school district. I was pregnant with our second child at the time, and his new position included a $10,000 pay raise. He essentially had the same job but was being paid significantly more.

Soon after he resigned, I was sitting in a leadership meeting with other teachers and administrators in my school district. I was still working in the same district that he had left. Somehow, I found myself seated directly next to the superintendent of the entire district. He knew about Matt's resignation, and during one of our meeting breaks, he turned to me, looked me straight in the eye, and asked, "What do I need to do to get Matt to stay with us?"

I wasn't expecting this question. He knew that it would be hard to replace Matt, especially in the summer months. I decided to be honest with him. What did I have to lose?

"You'd have to give him a raise. He took a $10,000 pay increase for this new job. Can you do that?"

He didn't even blink. "No, I can't."

I placed my hand on my stomach (I was almost eight months pregnant at this time) and responded, "Well, that pay increase covers this child's daycare cost. So if you can't give him a raise, then Matt won't be returning."

The superintendent ended the conversation, but at that moment, I realized how powerful a salary can be. Matt's ability to increase his income had a massive impact in our family. It allowed us to continue our debt-free journey while growing our family. It meant that we had less stress in our lives and more options when it came to our finances. The next year, I accepted a position in the same school district where Matt was working and took an $8,000 pay increase.

When it comes to decreasing your expenses or spending, you can only cut so much. That's why increasing your income will have the biggest impact on you meeting your money goals faster.

Increasing your income doesn't have to be complicated. Let's get into six ways you can increase your income so that you can speed up your money goals.

Ask for a Raise

If you haven't received a raise in the past year, then it might be time to ask for one. Before you schedule a meeting with your boss, do your prep work. Start by making a list of the projects you've worked on, the positive feedback you've received from clients, and any data or metrics highlighting how you've helped the company. Then, research the average salary for your job. This provides you and your boss with a clear example of what other companies in your area are paying for your specific role.

Search for a Higher-paying Job

One of the most effective ways to increase your salary is to accept a higher-paying position, usually at a different company. Switching jobs can be uncomfortable, because let's face it, change can be hard.

However, this is a great way to challenge yourself and enjoy a higher salary in the process.

Switch Careers Altogether

This might sound a little drastic, but hear me out. Sometimes switching careers altogether can make a dramatic difference for your income. If you're near the top of your pay ceiling in your current job, or if you are on a strict salary schedule, then it might be time to choose a career that has room for more growth. I've known someone who took a modest pay cut at her old job so that she could land an entry-level position at a new organization. Within two years her salary was higher than it would have been if she stayed in her old job. If this is something that you're interested in, think about the skill set you have, and start researching jobs that require that skill set. This is a great way to increase your income over the life of your career.

Start a Side Hustle

A side hustle, also called a side gig, is a way people make money in addition to their full-time job. It's a way of earning a supplemental income. This isn't the same as a part-time job. Most part-time jobs will have you clock in and clock out, and you have a set number of hours you must work, which really takes away from your freedom. With a side hustle, you set your own hours and earn as much or as little money as you have time to. When it comes to choosing a side hustle, think about the skills you already have. There's likely a way for you to turn your skill set into a full-blown side hustle.

Ask for More Hours at Work

If you're an hourly employee, you can easily increase your income by taking on more hours at work. Talk to your boss about what you can realistically work, and offer up your time in exchange for extra money. Even an extra five to ten hours each week can add up quickly.

Sometimes you can ask for extra responsibilities that include extra pay, such as training new employees for special types of work. Similarly, if you're specialized in technology, software, or methodology that your organization is going to start using, you could do a training seminar for a one-time bonus. Or you can offer to do some extra work that isn't already covered by anyone in the regular scheduled routine. Does the breakroom need painting? Are some lighting covers and wall fixtures covered with years of dust? Does anything need repairing? These can sometimes effectively be a side hustle within your regular job.

Work from Home

If you have a job where you work from a computer, then ask your boss about the possibility of working from home, even if it's just a few days each week. While this might not mean you'll earn extra money on your paycheck, it will decrease the amount of money you're spending on gas as well as the time you commute. This ultimately adds up to extra money in your bank account each month.

Think outside the Box

Increasing your income doesn't always look like extra money on your pay stub. Many jobs offer benefits or perks such as covered gym memberships or health care assistance. You can even look into mental health benefits such as free therapy sessions as well. Schedule an appointment with human resources to discuss the other perks that your job offers. These benefits can save you serious money, which frees up more cash flow to reach your goals quicker.

When it comes to reaching your money goals faster, you can't go wrong with decreasing your expenses or increasing your income. If you want to make even faster progress, do both.

Action Items

- Complete an expense audit on the following areas of your budget: housing, food, transportation, and insurance; and

- Choose one way you want to increase your income, and take action on it.

Chapter 12

How to Stay on Track with Your Money

People often struggle to stay on track with their budget and money goals. Sometimes people find themselves stuck in a cycle with their money.

In the beginning they set their budget up and look at it daily. It seems a little tight, but doable, and they feel empowered that their budget works on paper. But as time passes, life happens, unexpected expenses come up, and they don't know how to juggle these new money issues. They start to feel trapped, and a downward spiral begins. They become discouraged and stop checking their budget. They no longer know where they stand with their money. Then they start spending unbudgeted money and feel guilty and out of control. Finally, they work up the courage to start the cycle all over again. They feel empowered at the start of the cycle, but then new obstacles derail them again.

Can you relate to this cycle? Have you ever felt empowered starting out with your money only to feel like you have no control just weeks later?

This cycle is one that *many* people face. However, you *can* stay consistent when it comes to having control over your money and finances. You *can* stay on track with your money goals, even when life hands you unexpected expenses.

It's unrealistic to think that you'll never face bumps in the road while you're working on paying off debt, writing a budget that works, or building wealth. However, creating self-discipline with your finances and money habits can have a dramatic impact on your mindset and goals. This will help you stay on track and avoid the cycle described above.

What Is Self-discipline with Money?

Self-discipline with money looks like creating boundaries for your money based on your values and choosing to respect those boundaries every day.

Let's unpack this! First, it's important to create boundaries based on your own personal values. Some people have never set boundaries with their money from the very beginning. Other people create boundaries for their money based on what their family, friends, experts, or society in general says they should be doing. While it's okay to listen to input from those people, you ultimately need to determine for yourself what really works in the context of your life and goals.

Then, once you create your boundaries, you must agree to respect those boundaries each day. There's no doubt about it—sometimes respecting the money boundaries you set isn't as easy as it sounds.

However, when you have self-discipline with money, amazing things happen. When you have self-discipline with your money, you're able to:

- Create positive money habits that you can implement into your everyday life;
- Stay closer to your money goals; and
- Get back on track with your finances when an unexpected expense pops up.

Are you having a hard time with self-discipline even though you have the best intentions? There may be more than one reason why you could be struggling with sticking to the boundaries you create around money.

1. **Financial self-discipline was never modeled for you**. Self-discipline is a learned behavior, and if you have never seen it in action, how do you expect to apply it to your present life now?

2. **We live in a surplus world that distracts us from our money goals.** Unlimited options, choices, and opportunities make it hard to develop the self-discipline we need to say "no" when it comes to our spending habits.

3. **We want what we didn't have growing up.** If your parents were never able to afford a family vacation growing up, you may find it easier to justify spending money on a vacation for your own family, even if it means charging it to a credit card.

The big question is, How can you develop the financial self-discipline you need to stay on track to reach you money goals? Don't worry, it's possible, but it takes practice and intention.

Five Steps to Creating Self-discipline with Your Money

Last year our family gained a new family member: a sweet puppy that we lovingly named Harry. I had never had a puppy before, and while he brought an incredible amount of joy to our family, he also ushered in more frustration and stress than I care to admit.

Hands down, potty training that puppy was *much worse* than potty training either of my two children. I was the one at home with him, so my days were spent taking him outside every two hours while I held a treat and repeated the word "potty" until it no longer sounded like an actual word. While potty training felt like it lasted a full year, in reality, it only lasted a few weeks.

Looking back, I realize that both Harry and I had to learn more about discipline during this time. He had to learn how to ring a bell by our back door when he was ready to relieve himself, and I had to learn to have patience with what felt like never-ending accidents. Anyone who has potty trained a new puppy can relate. It takes effort, practice, and intention to teach a puppy how to stop using the bathroom on your living room rug. Thankfully, the time and energy it took helping Harry develop self-discipline was worth it.

Habits worth keeping require intention and practice. The same is true when it comes to creating discipline in your life, especially surrounding money. If you're unsure of *how* to go about creating self-discipline with money, don't worry. The five tips below will help you get started and be on the right track.

1. Make Learning a Priority

It's important to make learning about money and personal finance a priority in your life. Think of self-discipline as a foreign language. Would you ever move to a different country and suddenly find yourself speaking fluently in a foreign language you never knew before? Probably not. Instead, you would spend months, maybe even years, learning the new language through consistent practice and education. Then one day, the foreign language you've been practicing no longer feels foreign.

The same is true when it comes to developing self-discipline with your money. No one is born knowing how to handle money. It is something we all must learn. As you discover more about yourself and how you spend or save, you can also learn new habits. After you master sticking to a budget, keep learning about other financial situations.

Maybe ask yourself:

- What is investing?
- What counts as passive income?
- How can I work smarter, not harder?

Make learning about money a priority in your life. Read books like this one, listen to personal finance podcasts, and search the web. Do whatever it takes for you to learn and increase your knowledge when it comes to your money, and you'll start to develop the self-discipline that you didn't know was possible.

2. Look for Inspiration

When my husband and I were working to pay off debt, there were times that I wanted to give up on our goal. I knew this was a completely normal feeling and part of the process. I also knew that when I started to feel this way, I needed a little extra inspiration in my life. This is when I would scour the Internet for quotes that reminded me *why* I was working on changing our financial future. I'd binge podcast episodes that highlighted debt payoff success stories. I'd spend my free time searching for personal stories online that motivated me, and I made sure to follow people on social media that made me feel good.

To help create, and keep, self-discipline with your finances, think about what inspires and motivates you. Whether it's a simple quote or a success story you can relate to, let these inspirations encourage you as you continue your journey to financial freedom.

3. Create Boundaries That Feel Good to You

Discipline comes from setting and respecting the boundaries that you set in your life. Money boundaries are essentially a set of rules and expectations you follow when it comes to your money that help guide your decision-making. When we stick to our money boundaries, we make forward financial progress, which *feels good*.

One boundary that I've implemented in my life is to take 24 hours to "sleep" on any unplanned purchase that's over $100. If I didn't already have it in my budget, then that's my cue to take time before I spend money impulsively. This time allows me to think through *why* I want to make the purchase. It gives me an opportunity to decide whether I want to buy the item, add it to my next month's budget, or let go of the desire altogether. There have even been times that 24 hours later, I no longer want to buy it after all.

My husband and I have a similar boundary for large purchases such as appliances, vacations, and home upgrades. We take at least three days to think through the purchase before making a decision. These boundaries allow us to make money decisions based on facts and need, instead of impulsive desires. Take a moment to think about three boundaries that you'd like to set for yourself when it comes to your money.

4. Be Realistic

When we moved into our current home, we had boxes *everywhere*. If you've ever moved, you know that the unpacking process can take months. I was eager to be completely unpacked, so I set a goal to unpack every single box in a matter of seven days. I figured a full week was enough time to unpack, create a space for everything, and have our home "done."

Fast-forward seven days, and we still had boxes overflowing in our garage. Suddenly, I was frustrated with myself for not meeting the unrealistic seven-day expectation that I had set. Had I set realistic expectations for myself and my family from the beginning, I would not have been left feeling frustrated with myself. This is just one small example of how the expectations we set for ourselves need to be realistic.

Here's the truth: you will feel trapped if you create a set of unrealistic goals or expectations that you'll never be able to meet. Instead, choose to set realistic goals that will set you up for success over time. Start by setting goals that are *doable*. Let yourself achieve these small goals and let them motivate you to continue your money journey. And if you do find that you've set unrealistic goals, the answer is simple. Reset your goals to be realistic.

5. Find Ways to Motivate Yourself

This past summer our family spent a long weekend at one of our favorite Texas state parks. My husband and I love to hike, and every time we travel, we look for at least one hike to complete as a family. This time, my youngest son, James, was miserable, and a little over halfway through our hike, he decided he was done. After all my best "You can do it!" speeches fell flat, I knew it was time to go all in.

If you finish this hike, I'll buy you ice cream once we're done.

Yep, I went there. I bribed my son to finish our family hike. This external motivator was exactly what he needed to stand up and complete our trek to the top. While I would have loved for him to finish our family hike because it made him feel accomplished, that wasn't his reality. He needed something else, something extrinsic, to keep him going.

There will come a time when the same is true for you. When it comes to developing self-discipline with your money, there will be times when the feeling of pride, joy, and success keeps you moving forward. These internal, or intrinsic, motivators will be enough to keep you focused on your money goals.

However, there will also come a time when you will need an external, or extrinsic, motivator to keep you going. That's what James needed on our hike. He needed to have something to look forward to. He needed a prize when he crossed the finish line.

When you're starting to lose focus or feel yourself starting to give up on your money goals, give yourself an external motivator to work toward. This motivator can be as simple as a nice dinner out after you pay off your next loan. Or it could be planning a weekend away when you hit a financial milestone. Choose an external motivator that fits in your budget but also feels like a splurge, just like how James felt about a double scoop of chocolate ice cream.

Below is a list of internal and external motivators that my husband and I have used to stay on track with our budget and money goals.

Internal Motivators Examples

- Feeling less stressed about money;
- Having peace of mind with our bills;
- Freedom from debt payments;
- Having more options and choices with our money;
- Finally feeling confident and successful with money;
- Feeling security with our money and savings.

External Motivators Examples

- Family staycation when we hit a milestone;
- New outfit or shopping spree;
- Dinner out at our favorite restaurant;
- Snow cones with the kids;
- Couples vacation when we hit a big goal;
- Small home upgrades;
- Dinner out with friends.

Take a moment to brainstorm a list of possible internal and external motivators you can use to help you stay on track with your money when you are feeling stuck.

Tips to Stay on Track with Your Money

Sometimes it helps to have a few actionable tips that you can implement today to help you make progress with your money. The following tips can be implemented immediately and will help you stay on track with your budget and financial goals.

1. Keep Your Goals Visible

It's easy to get off track with your money when you forget what you're working toward. Living your life day-to-day can be a major distraction. To help you stay on track with your budget and money, keep your goals visible and refer to them often.

For example, if you want to be debt free, create a debt-free thermometer and keep it in a place you pass often. Make a point to think about and talk about your goals as much as possible with others who will cheer you on. When you start to get off track with your money or your goals, go to the visible representation you made. Fill it out and take time to reflect on the progress you've made. You'll find that you get very excited every time you get to cross something off the list, shade the thermometer, or close an account. That excitement quickly becomes motivation, and you'll find yourself getting closer and closer to your financial goals.

2. Create a Habit Tracker

One way to stay on track with your budget and money is to keep your money habits at the forefront of your mind. Creating a simple habit tracker is the perfect way to do this. Start by choosing two or three money habits that you'd like to track. Grab a calendar or list them in a journal. Every day you complete that habit, give yourself a checkmark or write the date down. I've even given myself a reward if I complete a habit 85% of the month.

Below are a few money habits you can start tracking today:

1. Categorize your expenses;
2. Think through purchases before you make a final decision;
3. Check in on your money or bank account balance;
4. Follow the meal plan you set.

I even like to add personal habits, such as exercising or drinking a certain amount of water to my habit tracker. In the end, a habit tracker acts as a reminder of how your daily habits can lead to big results.

3. Focus on What You Can Control

There are many outside factors that can have an impact on your personal finances. From rising inflation, to rent increases, to unexpected expenses that come up out of thin air—it's easy to feel like you are losing control over your money. While that can be frustrating, it's no reason to give up on your money goals.

Make it a priority in your life to focus on what you *can* control with your money. You likely have control over more than you even think. For instance, you can control the mindset you adopt around money. You have full control over your spending habits and whether you choose to budget. From setting aside money in an emergency fund to having money conversations with your partner, you are the one in control.

I have personally found that when I focus on what I can control in my life, especially when it comes to my finances, I show up with a positive attitude and a willingness to work toward my goals. Take a moment to think about three things you can control right now with your money. Write them down on a sticky note, and use this note as a reminder to focus on the ownership you have over your money.

4. Share Your Wins with Others

As I've emphasized earlier, it is crucial to have an accountability partner when you are trying to stick to a budget for the first (or fifth!) time. Your accountability partner can be a spouse, family member, or even a friend.

When you feel like giving up, or you need guidance, turn to your accountability partner for help and encouragement. Celebrate both your big and small wins with this person. Be honest and vulnerable when it comes to your struggles so they can encourage you. Having someone to walk with on this journey can make getting your money under control so much easier.

How Cash Can Change Everything

Before learning how to budget, I had the habit of spending money on whatever I wanted. I'd cross my fingers and hope that I would have money to last me until my next payday. Basically, I was winging it with my money. I honestly figured this was "good enough" for me and my future.

When our family started using cash envelopes, everything changed. Using cash envelopes gives you the opportunity to interact with your money and finances differently. It's no surprise that the cash envelope system has changed our finances and budget in several ways. It really has been a game-changing experience.

What Is the Cash Envelope System?

The cash envelope system is a way for you to take back control and track how much money you're spending on certain categories in your budget. Instead of using a debit card or credit card, you'll use cash for areas in your budget where you tend to overspend.

If you struggle with grabbing takeout or fast food too often, then you can have a cash envelope specifically for restaurants. Use the money you've set aside for restaurants any time you go out to eat. Once you've used up your budgeted amount, you won't have any cash left in your envelope. This helps keep you on budget and stay on track each month.

Why Cash Envelopes Help People Spend Less

Cash envelopes are not new. They have been used by people for years, and there's a reason why more and more people are using cash envelopes each day. Research shows that people overspend by

$7,400 each year. It's much easier to spend money when you're using a debit card or credit card. Handing over cash is harder. People have an emotional connection to physical money. It's more difficult to part with a $20 bill than it is to spend $20 on a debit card.

The number one reason why cash envelopes work is that they help you stay on track with your spending. The concept is simple. If you have $50 to spend on clothes, and you end up at the register with $57 worth of clothing, something must be put back. Using cash helps you develop better boundaries with your money. If you stay committed to only using the money that you budgeted for each cash envelope, then you will, without a doubt, stay on track each month financially.

How Cash Envelopes Work

Because I'm a teacher at heart and absolutely love step-by-steps, I'm breaking down how to use cash envelopes in easy-to-follow steps.

1. **Choose the categories you'll spend in cash.** Go back through your spending, and identify where you tend to over-spend. You can also consider using cash envelopes to save for sinking funds such as car maintenance or beauty expenses.

2. **Go to the bank and withdraw your cash.** Once you've made your budget, decide which denominations (hundreds, twenties, tens, fives, ones) you want in your envelopes. Make a tally sheet before you go to the bank so you know how much of each denomination you need to withdraw.

3. **Organize your money into your cash envelopes.** After you've pulled cash out from the bank, separate your money into cash envelopes. For instance, if you plan to spend $800

this month on groceries, then place eight one-hundred dollar bills in your envelope labeled "Groceries."

4. **Use your cash envelopes when you need them**. Take your cash envelopes with you when you need them. Once the money is gone, it's gone. This forces you to be intentional with your spending and will help you stay within the budget you set.

How Often Should You Withdraw Cash?

How often you are paid will help you determine how often you should withdraw money for your cash envelopes. For instance, if you are paid once a month, then it makes sense to withdraw money for your cash envelopes monthly. If you are paid biweekly, you might want to refill your cash envelopes every other week. The more you know your money and your budget, the easier it will be to determine how often you should refill your envelopes. If you're budgeting per paycheck, then it's probably best to pull out cash every paycheck. The key is to find what works for you.

Common Cash Envelope Categories

When I first heard about cash envelopes, I assumed that it meant you had to withdraw your *entire* paycheck in cash every month! Thankfully, this couldn't be farther from the truth. Instead of withdrawing cash for every category in your budget, only use cash envelopes for the areas in your budget where you tend to overspend. Not sure where you are spending too much money? That's okay. I recommend printing off your bank statements from last month. Go through each transaction and categorize it. Highlight all the transactions where you went out to eat in one color. Then use a different color highlighter

for all the times you ran to the grocery store. Once you've categorized your transactions, add up how much you're spending in each
area. If you're spending more than you had budgeted, then chances
are you could use a cash envelope for that category.

Below are common cash envelope categories:

- Food: groceries;
- Food: restaurants;
- Haircuts;
- Fun money;
- Entertainment;
- Clothing;
- Beauty/nails;
- Car maintenance (sinking fund);
- Home repairs (sinking fund);
- Christmas or holidays (sinking fund).

Ultimately, find what works for you when it comes to using cash
envelopes. My biggest tip is to start off small. Choose one or two
categories in your budget where you know you tend to overspend.
Try using cash envelopes for a few months in these two categories
before you add more cash envelopes to your life.

What to Do with Leftover Money

If you have extra money leftover at the end of the month, then let
me be the first one to congratulate you! Give yourself a pat on the
back and do a celebration dance. But what should you do with
that extra cash? Luckily, you have a few options on how to handle
leftover money.

- **Option 1:** Leave the extra money in your envelope. If you have any extra money in your restaurant envelope, one option is to leave it in your envelope and have even more money to spend the next month.

- **Option 2:** Leave the extra money in your envelope, but budget that much less the next month. Let's say you have $50 left in your restaurant envelope. If you normally budget $200 each month for eating out, this month you only need to budget $150 because you already have $50 in your cash envelope.

- **Option 3:** Send the extra money to savings. If you're trying to save up for a big purchase or vacation, then consider sending any leftover money from your cash envelopes to that savings account. This is a great way to stay motivated to spend even less than you would have planned.

- **Option 4:** Send the extra money to debt or another money goal. If you're on your debt-free journey, then consider taking any leftover cash and making an extra debt payment. This will help you make more progress on your debt journey or money goals.

What to Do If You Run Out of Money

What should you do if you run out of money in your cash envelopes before you can refill them? There have been several times when our cash envelope was empty before the next payday. Anytime this happened to me, I took it as a lesson learned.

If you run out of money, it's simple. You can't spend more money. Unlike using a credit card, you literally cannot buy anything if your cash envelope is empty. This is your budget's way of telling you that you're cut off. If you have $100 in your grocery envelope, you literally cannot spend more than $100. If your grocery bill is over $100, then you'll be forced to put something back.

Using cash envelopes helps hold you accountable to the budget you set. As long as you stick to using your cash envelopes, you will stay on budget. If you continue to run out of money month after month in a certain category, then it might be time to reevaluate your budget. Ask yourself if you're budgeting a realistic amount each month for that category. This might be a sign that it's time to increase how much you are budgeting for that category.

As always, the key to using cash envelopes is to find what works best for you. The more committed you are to the process, the greater your results. You never know, cash envelopes might be "the thing" that helps you stay on track with your budget and spending.

How to Get Back on Track with Your Money

Any time I end up going overboard with spending, I always do the same five things. I have a feeling these steps can help you get back on track with your money when you get off track.

1. Identify the Problem

You got off track with your budget or money for a reason. Something happened, or maybe something didn't happen. Regardless, you must be honest with yourself.

Ask yourself these questions to try and identify what went wrong:

- Were you trying to keep up with your friends and everything that they own?
- Were you unprepared for the month and didn't write out a budget?

- Did an unexpected expense pop up?
- Did you cave into impulse spending?

No matter what the problem was, it's important to identify it and face it. Be proactive and set up boundaries to prevent this problem from coming up again in the future. For instance, if an unexpected expense popped up, maybe it's time to set up a sinking fund for that expense. Or if you bought something "just because," then maybe it's time to deal with impulse spending. Once you have identified the problem, you can move forward financially.

2. Evaluate the Situation

The best way to move forward with your finances is to face your financial truth. This means you'll need to start tracking your expenses and be honest with where you stand with your finances and money. To get started, print your previous month's bank statement and evaluate your spending and money habits. Grab a calculator and total up how much you spent on unnecessary purchases.

Ask yourself the following questions to help you evaluate your current situation:

- How much debt do I have?
- Did I use a credit card unwisely while I was off track?
- Did I take money out of my savings to buy something I didn't need?
- What can I do moving forward to get back on track with my budget?

When you're able to evaluate your current situation, you know exactly where you stand so that you can take the next steps to move forward. Be honest with yourself about your money. Although this can be a difficult step to take, it is necessary if you want to move forward financially.

3. Make a Budget

If you are trying to turn your finances around, then it's time to make your budget a priority again. This tool can truly help get you back in shape. Budgeting doesn't have to be overwhelming. When you make budgeting a priority in your life, you might even look forward to writing a budget every paycheck. Budgeting allows you to be intentional about where you are sending your money.

If the idea of writing a budget makes you cringe, then try to make it fun. Turn it into a budget party by playing some music, eating your favorite snacks, and having a glass of wine (or two).

If you have a partner, be sure to include them fully when you're working on your budget.

4. Give Yourself Grace

No one is perfect. No matter how often you write a budget, chances are something unexpected will pop up. There will be times when you make an unplanned purchase. That's life! The truth is that even the most expert budgeters probably won't follow their budget perfectly.

Remember that your budget is a flexible document that can be changed at any point. When you're able to give yourself grace with your budget, you'll be more likely to continue budgeting every month. Giving yourself grace looks like letting go of any past money mistakes you've made and putting a plan in place moving forward.

5. Set New Goals

Once you've figured out why you've fallen off track with your money, you can set new goals in place to help hold you accountable to not go back down that road.

For instance, if you struggle with online shopping, then consider setting a goal to cut out any online shopping or Amazon shopping for an entire month. This type of reset allows you to see immediate progress and even gain back the confidence that you desire. When you set short-term goals, you are giving yourself an opportunity to make progress and prove to yourself that you're capable of achieving your goals.

Many people find themselves in the cycle of budgeting described at the beginning of this chapter. My hope is that you walk away from this book feeling confident to manage your money well. I hope that you feel empowered to face your finances and stay on track with your money goals. My hope is that you are working to build a strong financial foundation not just for this month, not just for this year, but for the rest of your life.

Action Items

- Choose one way that you will make learning about money a priority in your life. Some examples include reading about personal finance for 20 minutes each day or listening to an educational podcast about money.
- Create three boundaries that you'd like to set for yourself when it comes to your money. Examples include, "I will. . .
  - Wait 24 hours before spending money unplanned;
  - Track my spending every day;
  - Set rules around lending money to others;
  - Save 10% of my take home pay every month."
- Make a list of internal and external motivators to help you stay on track with your money goals.
- Use cash envelopes for your spending in one or two categories of your budget.

Chapter 13

Investing for Your Future

During the first five years of our money journey, paying off debt and setting up an emergency fund was our sole focus. At that time, my husband and I didn't have the desire or know-how when it came to investing. Retirement felt like a world away, so we put it off to work on "later."

"Later" eventually came, and to be completely honest, we were way outside of our comfort zone. We had never learned about investing in the past. Between the complicated vocabulary and fear of losing all our money, we lacked the confidence to be the people in charge of our retirement. That's when we decided to hand over our investing responsibility to a financial planner.

We had someone help us with investing for a few years before we realized that the fees we were being charged would add up to a *lot* of money over the years. What would start out as pennies would eventually amass to thousands upon thousands of dollars over time. When Matt and I realized this, we decided that it was time to learn about investing: how it works, what our options are, and how to keep it simple.

As it turns out, I'm not alone when it comes to learning about investing. According to a study by Fidelity in 2021, 64% of women *want* to be more active in their investment decisions. But something is holding them back: confidence. Fidelity found that only 31% of women feel confident planning for financial needs in retirement.

It's easy to put off a task when you lack the confidence and know-how to make it happen. Investing is no different. The only way to feel confident about a topic such as investing is to face it head on: make it one of your priorities to learn about investing and ask questions. As it turns out, there's no better time to start learning than now!

Your Step-by-step Investing Plan

I asked over 800 people the same question: *What's holding you back from investing?*

Almost all the responses I received boiled down to the same concern: *I don't know how to invest, and I don't want to do the wrong thing.*

We've heard it time and time again—you need to invest for your future. But what does that look like? And how do you make it happen?

If you're new to investing, the vocabulary alone can be intimidating. Thankfully, investing doesn't have to be complicated for the average person. When you have a system or plan to follow, investing can be, dare I say it, *easy*! Let's break down investing into steps that will make it less intimidating for you.

1. Think Ahead to Your Future

Before we dive into the actual steps to invest your money, it's important to establish *why* investing is important to you. What we do today determines the peace of mind we have in our future. For me, peace of mind looks like being able to afford the lifestyle I want when I'm no longer working. Peace of mind looks like being able to travel to see my kids or future grandkids. It looks like being able to confidently afford doctor's visits or health care. Peace of mind looks like having the money I need to live a comfortable life during retirement.

Take 10 minutes to think about *why* you want to get started with investing for retirement. What do you want to do when you retire?

How do you want to feel when it comes to your money? What do you want your average day to look like? Getting clear on this will help you stay focused and make investing for your future a priority in your life.

2. Do the Math

The first time I ever did the math to determine how much money I would need to have set aside to retire comfortably, I immediately thought, "What's wrong with this calculator? It must be broken." So naturally, I punched the numbers in the calculator a second time. I was shocked to see the same number pop up on my calculator. Eventually, the shock wore off, and I reminded myself that I had *time* to build my wealth. The same is true for you.

To get a good idea of how much money you'll need to save for retirement, it all comes down to (yep, you might have guessed it) your budget. Start by figuring out how much money you'll need monthly when you retire. You can think of this as your "retirement budget." Of course, you don't have a crystal ball, so you won't know *exactly* how much your expenses will be down to the penny. However, even coming up with a decent estimate is a great starting point.

When making your monthly retirement budget, be sure to include:

- Living expenses;
- Travel;
- Money for fun;
- Money for giving;
- Medical expenses.

Now that you have an idea of what you'll spend monthly when you retire, multiply that number by 12 months to determine your yearly expenses.

For example, if you think you'll need $6,000 each month, then your formula would look like this:

$$\$6,000 \text{ monthly expenses} \times 12 \text{ months} = \$72,000 \text{ annual expenses}.$$

Essentially, you'll need to withdraw $72,000 each year out of your investments to be able to live comfortably. To determine how much your entire nest egg should be, multiply your annual expenses by 25. Let's continue with the example from above:

$$\$72,000 \text{ annual expenses} \times 25 = \$1,800,000.$$

This means your goal is to save $1,800,000 for retirement. Sounds like a lot, right? Fortunately, compound interest plays a massive role when it comes to saving for retirement.

3. Understand How Investing Works

Okay, so you have an idea of *how much* money you'll need to retire, but how on earth are you supposed to get that money? Enter: the stock market!

Simply put, the stock market typically refers to the buying and selling of shares (or portions of shares) of publicly held companies.

The more technical definition according to Investopedia.com, reads: stock markets are venues where buyers and sellers meet to exchange equity shares of public corporations. Stock markets are components of a free-market economy because they enable democ-ratized access to investor trading and exchange of capital.

For simplicity's sake, it's important to know that the stock market refers to the buying and selling process of stocks, bonds, and other assets. This means that:

- Companies list shares of their stock (or small pieces of ownership of their company) on the stock exchange;
- Investors (like me and you) can purchase those shares, meaning we own a very small portion of that company;
- Investors can buy and sell these stocks among each other.

Investors have tracked the stock market for *years* on end. In fact, the stock market return has been on average about 10% each year for the last 100 years. Of course each year the rate of return fluctuates, but over time it averages out to be about 10%. The fact that the stock market fluctuates over time can tell us that it's meant for long-term investments, meaning, you put your money in the stock market and let compound interest do its job for as long as possible.

Compound interest is the interest (the money you earn) on both your original deposit *and* on the interest that your money earns.

Let's look at an example of compound interest in action. Let's say that you invest $6,000 each year (which comes out to $500 each month) starting at the age of 30. Even with an estimated interest rate of 7%, by the time you are 65, you will have $887,481 in your investment account. The best part is that you only had to contribute $210,000 over the years, and compound interest did the rest of the work for you.

Table 13.1 Compound Interest Example

Age	Total Contributions	Rate of Return (7%)	Total
30	$6,000.00	$420.00	$6,420.00
31	$12,000.00	$869.40	$13,289.40
32	$18,000.00	$1,350.26	$20,639.66
33	$24,000.00	$1,864.78	$28,504.44
34	$30,000.00	$2,415.31	$36,919.75
35	$36,000.00	$3,004.38	$45,924.13
36	$42,000.00	$3,634.69	$55,558.82
37	$48,000.00	$4,309.12	$65,867.94
38	$54,000.00	$5,030.76	$76,898.70
39	$60,000.00	$5,802.91	$88,701.61
40	$66,000.00	$6,629.11	$101,330.72
41	$72,000.00	$7,513.15	$114,843.87
42	$78,000.00	$8,459.07	$129,302.94
43	$84,000.00	$9,471.21	$144,774.15
44	$90,000.00	$10,554.19	$161,328.34
45	$96,000.00	$11,712.98	$179,041.32
46	$102,000.00	$12,952.89	$197,994.21
47	$108,000.00	$14,279.59	$218,273.80
48	$114,000.00	$15,699.17	$239,972.97
49	$120,000.00	$17,218.11	$263,191.08
50	$126,000.00	$18,843.38	$288,034.46
51	$132,000.00	$20,582.41	$314,616.87
52	$138,000.00	$22,443.18	$343,060.05
53	$144,000.00	$24,434.20	$373,494.25
54	$150,000.00	$26,564.60	$406,058.85
55	$156,000.00	$28,844.12	$440,902.97
56	$162,000.00	$31,283.21	$478,186.18
57	$168,000.00	$33,893.03	$518,079.21
58	$174,000.00	$36,685.54	$560,764.75
59	$180,000.00	$39,673.53	$606,438.28
60	$186,000.00	$42,870.68	$655,308.96
61	$192,000.00	$46,291.63	$707,600.59
62	$198,000.00	$49,952.04	$763,552.63
63	$204,000.00	$53,868.68	$823,421.31
64	$210,000.00	$58,059.49	$887,480.80

Table 13.1 shows how your money would grow over time if invested. The first column is your age, the second column shows

your total contributions, the third column is your rate of return, and the last column is your total (your contributions plus interest earned).

Isn't that amazing? You contributed $210,000 to your retirement account and earned over $677,480 alone in interest! All for having your money in the stock market. The power of compound interest allows your money to grow over time, can help you reach your long-term money goal, and is a key in building wealth.

Seeing compound interest in action made me want to jump at the chance of investing my money. I hope it does the same for you. I recommend you take time to insert your own numbers into a compound interest calculator. Investor.gov has a great calculator that allows you to change your monthly contributions to help you determine how much money you'll need to invest each month to reach your target retirement goal. They also have a calculator in Spanish for any Spanish speakers.

4. Choose the Right Account for You

Whether you have retirement on your mind or not, you will want to consider retirement accounts. Most of these account types allow you to pick and choose your investments. Just remember—money sitting in an account doesn't do anything until you invest it.

The right account for you will depend on your current job, income level, and how much money you are able to invest each year. Below is a list of common retirement account options.

- **401(k)** is an is an employer-sponsored retirement plan. If you're lucky enough to have one, you should use it. With it, you can dedicate a certain amount of your pre-tax salary to the account. Some employers will even offer to match your contributions. Did someone say free money? With your 401(k), you can invest in stocks, bonds, and mutual funds, which the employee can select. The account will be managed by an investment company that the employer chooses.

- **403(b) plan**, also known as a tax-sheltered annuity plan, is a retirement plan specifically created for employees of public schools and other tax-exempt organizations such as state colleges, universities, and church employees. Your contributions will be withdrawn directly from your paycheck through a payroll deduction.

- **457** is like a 401(k) plan but is specifically for employees at state or local government levels. The most common type of 457 is a 457(b), which is tax deferred. This means that contributions are taken out of your paycheck pre-tax. A 457 also offers people close to retirement age an opportunity to catch up by contributing double the normal limit.

- **TSP**, short for Thrift Savings Plan, is only offered to federal employees and members of uniformed services. This plan is similar to a 401(k) plan. For anyone with a TSP, you have six options, or funds, when it comes to investing.

- **Solo 401(k)** was designed specifically for small business owners. Also known as a self-employed 401(k), the Solo 401(k) is perfect for those who own their own business but do not have any employees. With a Solo 401(k), you can make contributions both as the employee as well as the employer. They have become popular and are relatively easy to set up.

- **SEP IRA** is short for Simplified Employee Pension IRA. This is like a Solo 401(k) but was created for small business owners and their employees. A SEP IRA is simple to set up and has higher contribution limits than a traditional IRA.

- **Traditional IRA** is a type of individual retirement account. With traditional IRA accounts, you contribute money before it's been taxed. The money then grows tax deferred. After the age of 59½, you can make withdrawals, but they will be taxed as income.

- **Roth IRA** is a type of individual retirement account. Unlike a traditional IRA, a Roth IRA allows you to make contributions after your money has already been taxed. The money then grows tax-free, and you can withdraw without needing to pay tax after age 59½. Sounds too good to be true, right? Well, it isn't! There is a contribution limit as well as an income limit for the Roth IRA. These limits change every few years, but you can find the limits for the current year with a simple online search.

- **HSA** is a health savings account. An HSA can help pay for out-of-pocket medical costs, but it may surprise you to learn that this tax-advantaged account could be a superior retirement savings vehicle, too. To qualify for an HSA, you must have a high-deductible insurance plan and not yet qualify for Medicare.

- **Taxable Brokerage Account** has no tax benefits but offers more flexibility when it comes to investing. There is no limit on how much money you can invest in a taxable brokerage account. However, whatever you invest will be taxed when you withdraw the money. Unlike other accounts, you can withdraw your money at any time and at any age. When you withdraw the money, you'll be subject to capital gains tax. Thankfully, if you hold onto your investments for longer than a year, you'll pay long-term capital gains tax, which tends to be lower than short-term capital gains tax.

Once you know which retirement account (remember, you can have more than one) is best for you, it's time to open your account. Start by sitting down with someone from human resources to discuss your options. Most accounts can also be opened very easily online.

5. Buy Your Investments

Now that you have your accounts open, the fun begins: it's time to purchase your investments. A very common investing mistake is to open a retirement account and stop there. After opening the account, you must transfer money into your account and buy the investments you're interested in.

But what on earth should you buy? The five most common investments include stocks, bonds, mutual funds, index funds, and ETFs.

- **Stock**: When you think of investing, you probably think of stocks. A stock is a tiny ownership of a company—think of it as your mini slice of a greater pie. The cost of individual stocks depends on the share price and can range from a few dollars to thousands. Stocks are the most intimidating and difficult investment to learn for beginners. You can handpick individual stocks, but this takes lots of time, effort, and money. As a general rule of thumb, never invest in something you don't fully understand.

- **Bond**: Bonds are the other commonly known, much tamer sister to stocks. Essentially, bonds are a type of contract where you lend money to some entity with the promise that they will pay you back with interest. Most are corporate, municipal, or US Treasury bonds (T-Bonds). Bonds are considered very safe and predictable—you know exactly how much money you're giving out and the amount of interest it will accrue. As a little bonus, the interest earned from government bonds is not taxed. But with less risk comes less reward. You're going to get a significantly lower rate of return for them. Bonds are a great option for those with a specific timeline on their money. Young people should aim for investments for growth rather than only buying bonds. They're also part of a well-balanced portfolio.

- **Mutual Fund**: Mutual funds allow you to get involved with investing when you don't feel like putting in the research or want something with little effort on your end. Mutual funds are when a portfolio manager pools the money of different investors together and purchases different assets. Essentially, you're buying into a portfolio of stocks, bonds, indexes, ETF funds, and more. You provide the money, and someone else will oversee it. Mutual funds are a very popular investment but are slowly falling out of favor. They have high fees known as management expense ratio (MER). In the US, 1% is a common MER you will see. It might not sound like much, but it can really take a chunk of your money over time

- **Index Fund**: Similar to mutual funds, index funds are not selecting individual assets but instead investing in a pool of assets. With index funds, you are trying to track a market index. A market index is the overall performance of a particular industry. Index funds try to mirror the performance of the overall stock market by buying the stocks in a particular index. For instance, you've probably heard of the S&P 500. An index fund that tracks the S&P 500 holds the stock of all the largest companies in the US. This is a passive approach to investing and doesn't require much tracking on the investors' part—computers and algorithms do most of the work. This makes index funds a much cheaper option with fewer fees.

- **ETF**: Exchange-traded funds (ETFs) are often lumped together with index funds. They also follow the whole stock market by investing in a sample of the most common stocks. They roll along with the market rather than try to beat it. The only main difference between ETFs and index funds is that they are traded throughout the day and purchased at a share price, which can fluctuate throughout the day.

Before you invest, do your due diligence. Only invest in what you fully understand.

6. Set Yourself Up for Success

Now that you know the common types of investments available to you, it's time to make an investment plan that aligns with your goals and personal situation. Here's what you need to consider before you invest.

- **Understanding risk**: Some investments are going to be riskier than others. So consider how comfortable you are with risk and whether or not you are in a position to be risky. For instance, someone with children and a mortgage is less likely to be risky than an independent person renting a home. More often than not, the risk is all about finding the right balance. You need some risk to grow your money, but you also don't want to lose it all.

- **Identifying your goals**: Everyone has a different time frame. Younger people who begin investing have much more time to grow their money. They have more freedom to be risky as they wait out the ups and downs of the market. Investing early gives you an edge. Investing has a snowball effect as you earn money on the money your investments have already earned. That's the joy of compounding! On the other hand, older people can't jeopardize their nest egg and ability to retire. While they may have patience, they must figure out a realistic way to maintain their money.

- **Diversifying your investments**: Never put all your eggs in one basket. Instead, always spread your money across various investments—this helps to reduce investment risk. This means investing in different forms of investments such as stocks and bonds, different industries, and different markets. Mix high- and low-risk investments. This ensures your investments grow, but you won't ever be at risk of losing everything.

Remember, it doesn't matter how much money you have; the important thing is just to get started. This will set you up for success down the road as you slowly can contribute more to investing.

Investing While in Debt

I think we can agree that investing is a good idea—when you have the money to invest. But what if you feel stuck because you still have debt payments lingering around? (I'm looking at you, student loans.) Is it still a good idea to invest?

Well, maybe. It is possible to invest while paying off debt, and it can be beneficial too. Looking into the future and thinking of retirement can feel daunting when you are also working to pay off debt. You might feel like if you don't immediately start to invest while paying off debt, you'll never have enough when the time comes. But, on the other hand, you may not feel sure about taking money away from paying off debt to invest it. This concern is totally valid. You aren't alone.

The good news is that you can invest while paying off debt. Here are some things to consider if you want to invest while paying off debt.

1. Compare Earned Interest vs. Owed Interest

Perhaps the most crucial thing you must discover as you decide whether to invest while paying off debt is what you stand to lose and gain. You owe interest on your debt, and you also want to earn interest on your investment. The immediate issue most consumers run into is that interest on debt is typically much higher in general than the interest you can earn on investing, especially if you are battling credit card debt. This is important to factor in because you could be losing much more in the short term than you gain in the long term if you don't take the time to get your math right.

For example: If you are making a minimum credit card payment on a $5,000 balance at 24% interest (probably about $200 per month), it will take you 36 months to pay off that debt in full. Over the course of those 36 months, you'll have paid an extra $2,000 in interest alone.

Now let's say you decide to invest $200 each month in an index fund that tracks the total stock market for thirty-six months. Over the last 100 years, the stock market has returned on average 10% each year. But let's be conservative and assume an 7% return on your investments. In 36 months, your investments would be worth about $7,715. Your total contribution would be $7,200 and the interest you gained would be $515.

In this case, you might be better off paying down your credit card as soon as you possibly can, preferably much sooner than the 36 months used in this example. This way, you will pay less over time in interest to the credit card company leaving you more money to invest each month. A good rule of thumb is to pay off your high-interest debt as soon as possible and then start investing.

2. Learn How to "Pay Yourself" Responsibly

Investing when it is practical to do so is always a good idea, whether or not you are paying off debt. In a world where high risk yields high rewards, it's easy to try and shoot for the moon, but the best approach is always to be responsible with your cash flow. Budget your money well so that you know who's getting paid what and when each debt will be paid off. When you can project an accurate timeline for when your debt will go away, and you have room in that plan to set money aside, you could and should invest that money in your future by any practical means.

3. Establish and Maintain an Emergency Fund

Before getting into anything resembling compound interest, I think one of the top things you should consider when you want to invest while paying off debt is your emergency fund. When you are on the road to being debt free, there are always obstacles that seem to jump in your way just when you think you're getting a grip. As frustrating as it is, it's just a fact of life.

Emergency funds are meant to give you a cushion so you don't have to go into debt to cover unexpected expenses or job loss. If you find yourself regularly dipping into your emergency fund to make ends meet, you may not be ready to invest. Try to accumulate at least a few months' worth of income, and make sure you can keep that safety net in place before using additional funds to invest.

4. Make Investing a Priority

Once you decide when and how to invest, that investment in your-self must be treated as seriously as debt. Make sure you prioritize those payments and keep on top of them. The more you put in now, the more you will have access to once you're in retirement. However, only invest what is reasonable.

If you bite off more than you can chew, that investment will not be sustainable, and you will have to shift your priorities once again. Find a good stable level of investment that you can comfortably commit to for the next several years.

With a little planning and effort, you can pay off debt and invest too.

Investing Tips

There are two ways to make money. The first way is what you're likely already doing: working your normal full-time job. The second way to earn money is to put your money to work by investing in the stock market. Investing allows you to increase your income and build wealth without spending more of your *time* working.

You will always hear me preaching this message: Everybody, no matter your age, should be saving for retirement. No longer can we depend on earning a pension for our retirement. Retirement requires a hefty amount of money to ensure you maintain the same standard of living. The last thing you want is to be working longer than you should.

Follow the Simple Formula

When it comes to building wealth, there's a simple formula to follow in life.

Spend Less than You Make + Invest the Extra + Avoid Debt = Retire without Stress.

When you're able to focus on these three things and practice them consistently, you'll set yourself up to retire comfortably. From this moment on, focus on doing these three things.

1. **Spend less than you make:** your expenses should never be more than your take-home pay. If they are, it's time to either earn more money or cut back on your spending (or both).
2. **Invest the extra:** If you are spending less money than you make, you should have extra cash every month. Make it a priority in your life to invest the extra money you have each

month. Do you have to invest all of it? Maybe not, but investing your extra money consistently will help multiply your money. Find a balance that works for you.

3. **Avoid debt:** If you already have debt, vow to work on paying it off and not taking on any new debt if you can avoid it.

When you're able to live by this formula, you'll feel relieved, empowered about your money, and excited for your future.

Invest Early and Consistently

Once you understand how investing in the stock market works, it's important to start investing as early as possible. The sooner you start investing, the more time your money has to grow thanks to compound interest.

You might be thinking that you shouldn't invest if you can't send a significant amount of money to retirement each month. What if you don't have an extra $500 each month to send to your 401(k)? That's okay. When I first started investing, I was focused on contributing just $100 each month toward my Roth IRA. Over time I was able to increase my contributions so I can meet my retirement goals.

The goal isn't to wait until you have the *perfect* amount of money to invest each month. The goal is to start investing as early as possible and consistently over time, even if that looks like investing $50 each month. It's easy to set up automatic contributions through your 401(k) or IRA. This simple act will make investing a standard habit in your life.

Keep Your Fees Low

Fees can have a big impact on how much wealth you can build, so it's important to minimize your fees as much as you can. Think

265

Investing for Your Future

of it this way: the less fees you pay, the more of your money you get to keep.

Mutual funds, index funds, and ETFs charge an expense ratio. This is essentially the cost you'll pay to a company for managing those funds. The lower the expense ratio, the lower your fees. Index funds have a history of low fees, some as low as 0.03%. Actively managed mutual funds tend to have higher fees, sometimes upward of 1.5%. While 1.5% might not sound like a high fee, this compounds over time. Thankfully for you and me, fees have been on the decline over the past 20 years. Before you buy any funds, always check the expense ratio *first*.

Take a Long-term Approach to Investing

Nothing in life is guaranteed. The same is true when it comes to the stock market. We've all heard the horror stories of people losing money in the stock market, especially when a recession hits. However, it's important to zoom out and look at the big picture when it comes to investing. There will be ups and downs in the market; this is perfectly normal and to be expected. But if you look at the average return of the stock market over the last 100 years, you'll see that the stock market returns on average about 10% per year. Investing doesn't have to be complicated or even exciting. In fact, it can be simple and boring when you're willing to take a long-term approach to investing.

Retirement Comes before College

The first time I took one of my children on an airplane, my son was only eight months old. I remember sitting in my seat before takeoff, and the flight attendant walked up to me with a safety card in hand. She leaned in toward me, looked me dead in the eyes, and told me that in case of an emergency I needed to put my oxygen mask on first and *then* place an oxygen mask on my son.

The logical part of me understood why I was being told to do this, but the emotional side of me was adamant against it. *Why would I put myself before my child? That's absurd! I'll always put my child's needs before my own!*

Thankfully, I've never been in a situation where I had to put an oxygen mask on in a plane. However, like other parents out there, I'm currently in a similar situation when it comes to saving for my children's college. *Should saving for your kid's college come before saving for your retirement?*

After some thought, my husband and I decided to prioritize our retirement goals over saving for our kid's college fund. Essentially, we are putting our oxygen masks on first and then taking care of the kids. Now, don't get me wrong. We love our kids dearly and want the best for them. In a perfect world, we would be able to pay for their entire college in full. But we also don't want them to have to take care of us when we are older. We don't want them to have to help their parents out because we didn't plan for retirement in advance. It all comes down to this one simple truth: *you can't take out loans for retirement.*

Because of this, we are currently contributing over three times as much money to our retirement accounts compared to their college fund. When, or if, our kids do choose to attend college, we hope they still don't have to take out student loans. Here's our current plan:

1. Use the money we have saved in their 529 college savings accounts;

2. Include a portion of college expenses in our monthly budget when our children enter college;

3. Require our kids to apply for scholarships;

4. Require our kids to get a part-time job to help cover living expenses.

If our kids must take out student loans after all four of these plans are in place, then hopefully they will be minimal. In the meantime, we are trying our best to invest as much as we can toward our retirement so that we set ourselves and our kids up for a better future.

When it comes to your own retirement plans, make sure that you are prioritizing your retirement plans *before* saving for your kids' college. If you have more money left over each month to set aside for your kids, great. If not, that's okay. Your children have options when it comes to receiving a higher education.

Action Items

- Think about *why* you want to make investing a priority in your life. What do you want to do when you retire? How do you want to feel when it comes to your money? What do you want your average day to look like?

- Determine how much money you'll need yearly during retirement. Take that yearly amount and multiply it by 25 to find your retirement goal amount.

- Go to investor.gov and use their compound interest calculator to determine how much money you'll need to invest each month to reach your target retirement goal.

- Choose the right investment accounts for you. Schedule a meeting with HR if you have an employer.

- Research and purchase your investments.

- Live by the following formula:

Spend Less than You Make + Invest the Extra + Avoid Debt = Retire without Stress.

Chapter 14

Conclusion

Congratulations! You made it to the end of this book. You deserve to be celebrated. Why? Because the fact that you're here, reading this book, shows that you are prioritizing your money and finances. You're willing to put in the effort to write a budget that works, pay off debt, and create financial habits that will change your life.

Budgeting and making your money a priority can make money *easy,* even when in the past it was anything but simple. Prioritizing your finances can help you reach goals that in the past felt impossible.

It all starts with intention.

It all starts with a budget.

It starts with being willing to do something *different* from what you were doing before.

I have no doubt that you will gain confidence as you implement the steps in this book.

1. **Find your catalyst.** No matter what your catalyst may be, hold it close to your heart. It will be *the* driving force that will get you started and keep you motivated as you learn how to manage your money better.

2. **Adopt a positive money mindset and money habits.** Your money mindset matters—today, tomorrow, and years from now. Do the work to change your outlook on money, and implement positive money habits into your everyday life.

3. **Write a budget that works.** Your budget gives you the opportunity to be intentional with your money. It gives you the freedom to prioritize what you value most. The more specific and realistic your budget, the easier it will be to stick to it.

4. **Implement the secrets behind successful budgeting.** Write a mini-budget when you get off track with your finances. It will be a game changer in your life.

5. **Pay off debt.** Choose a debt payoff plan to help you pay off debt while enjoying life along the way.

6. **Save for emergencies.** An emergency fund safeguards your finances so that you can still work toward your money goals when unexpected events occur. Save at least three months of necessary expenses in an emergency fund.

7. **Set up sinking funds.** Choose a few sinking funds to add to your budget. They will help you plan in advance for large purchases or unexpected mishaps.

8. **Create money goals.** Specific and measurable goals will help you experience success. The best way to set and reach your goals is to start with the end in mind and work your way back from there.

9. **Conquer impulse spending.** Determine the real reason behind your impulse spending. Then, create boundaries to help you be successful with your money and avoid impulse spending.

10. **Work with your partner.** Communicating with your spouse about money is much more than just talking about money. It's laying a solid foundation of teamwork and grace for your relationship, your family, and generations to come.

11. **Accelerate your financial progress.** If you're willing to sacrifice for a *season*, you can live the rest of your life in *abundance*. No matter whether you want to accelerate a short-term goal or a long-term goal, every dollar counts. Find ways to speed up your financial progress, even if it's just temporary.

12. **Stay on track with your money.** Actively practice self-discipline with your money. Self-discipline surrounding money can help you stay on track with your finances, even when faced with unexpected expenses.

13. **Invest for your future.** Make investing a priority in your life. Start early and invest consistently over time.

You have everything you need to take the next step toward reaching financial freedom. All you need to do is start exactly where you are. Come back to this book and refer to it often. Let it be a reminder of what you are working toward in your life.

Above all, remember that you are on your own unique journey. It won't look like anyone else's, and that's okay. Find joy in the lessons, let them empower you, and share your success with others along the way.

I'd love for you to stay connected as well! You can reach me at www.inspiredbudget.com or @InspiredBudget on social media. I cannot wait to hear what you've learned as well as the success you've experienced. I'm here to cheer you on along the way!

All the best,
Allison

About the Website

You can find this book's worksheets and tools to help you gain control of your money and manage your finances at www.inspiredbudget.com/moneymadeeasy, including:

- Catalyst for Change Worksheet (Chapter 1)
- My Money Truth Worksheet (Chapter 2)
- Bill Payment Log (Chapter 3)
- Budget Page (Chapter 3)
- My Debt Payoff Plan Worksheet (Chapter 5)
- Emergency Fund Page (Chapter 6)
- Sinking Funds: What I Know Will Happen Worksheet (Chapter 7)
- Sinking Funds: What I Want to Happen Worksheet (Chapter 7)
- Sinking Funds: What Might Happen Worksheet (Chapter 7)
- Sinking Funds: How Much to Save Worksheet (Chapter 7)
- Sinking Funds Location Worksheet (Chapter 7)
- Review the Goal Worksheet (Chapter 8)
- Yearly Goals Worksheet (Chapter 8)
- Impulse Spending Worksheet (Chapter 9)

Index

279